The Letters of Herbert Kelly SSM and Dorothy L. Sayers 1937-1947

Edited by Scholastica Jacob

Society of the Sacred Mission
Durham

Published by The Society of the Sacred Mission

St Antony's Priory
74 Claypath
Durham
DH1 1QT
United Kingdom
www.ssm.org.uk

ISBN: 978-1-0687286-0-0

CONTENTS

Acknowledgments

I am grateful to Laura Stanifer, archivist at the Marion E. Wade Center, Wheaton College, Wheaton, IL for her help in locating material in the Sayers archive, checking the dates of letters and providing the photographs of Dorothy L. Sayers and the Archangels.

My thanks also go to the staff at the Borthwick Institute, York who look after the SSM archives and for the excellent quality scans of photographs in this book.

Finally, this project would not have been possible without the support of the Trustees of SSM, and Nicholas Buxton, Director of St Antony's Priory, not least in the editorial process of bringing the manuscript to publication.

List of Illustrations

Herbert Kelly in his study at Kelham, 1930s (SSM Archives)

Dorothy L. Sayers, c. 1938, photograph by Howard Coster (Used by permission of the Marion E. Wade Center, Wheaton College, Wheaton, IL, USA)

Scene from the performance of Zeal of Thy House, Canterbury Cathedral, 1937. Photograph by W. Fisk-Moore, Canterbury (Used by permission of the Marion E. Wade Center, Wheaton College, Wheaton, IL, USA)

High Mass in the Great Chapel at Kelham (SSM Archives)

Facsimile of the original letter from Herbert Kelly to Dorothy L. Sayers, 10 October 1940 (SSM Archives)

Facsimile of the original letter from Dorothy L. Sayers to Herbert Kelly 15 May 1941 (SSM Archives)

Foreword

This volume represents one of the first fruits of an exciting new initiative that has been developed by the Society of the Sacred Mission at St Antony's Priory in Durham, namely the establishment of an Institute for Anglican Religious life.

The purpose of this is twofold. First, to ensure the preservation of the legacy of Anglican religious life, at a critical juncture when many communities are in decline. This entails determining the whereabouts of archives, as well as supporting communities in developing catalogues and securing the long-term future of their collections.

But it's not just about the past. The second element concerns the future of Anglican religious life. Even though traditional forms of religious life appear to be on the wane, the call to holiness remains universal and constant. How can we resource those seeking to answer that call?

It is thus intended that the Institute will become a centre of gravity for all things related to Anglican religious life.

And so to this volume, which brings together for the first time the full correspondence between Fr Herbert Kelly, founder of SSM, and the celebrated novelist and playwright, Dorothy L. Sayers. The letters have been skilfully edited by Dr Scholastica Jacob, and are presented here with a wealth of detailed footnotes and an illuminating introduction, which provides valuable context as well as informative discussion of a number of salient themes.

We hope it will be followed by many more works drawing on the untapped treasures of religious archives.

Revd Dr Nicholas Buxton, St Antony's Priory

INTRODUCTION

This volume contains the correspondence between Anglican priest and theologian, Herbert Hamilton Kelly of the Society of the Sacred Mission (SSM) and crime novelist, playwright, and Christian apologist, Dorothy L. Sayers. These lively letters cover the years 1937 to 1947 and provide a commentary on social and religious developments in the immediate pre-war and war years as well as insight into the thoughts and theology of two innovative and creative minds. The name of Sayers is well known today, most especially for her detective novels but also for her spiritual essays and dramas. Kelly is less well known outside Anglican circles.

Herbert Kelly was born in Manchester on 18 July 1860. He was the third of seven children born to James Devonport Kelly and his wife Margaret. James Kelly, a 'steady Evangelical', was a rector and later canon of Manchester Cathedral.[1] The eldest son, Arthur, joined the army and the second, Francis, Herbert's 'chum brother', died while Herbert was at Oxford. His 'chum sister', Edith, went on to become a member of the Community of the Epiphany, and spent many years as a missionary in Japan. The

---

[1] George Every (ed.), *Herbert Kelly, No Pious Person: Autobiographical Recollections* (London: Faith Press, 1960), p. 20.

youngest brother, Alfred Davenport, was to follow Herbert's lead and join SSM in 1900.

By his own admission, Kelly had a less than illustrious academic career. The deafness he suffered from childhood, and which became increasingly more severe with age, was a contributing factor.[2] He was educated first at Manchester Grammar School and then followed his brother Arthur to the Royal Military Academy, Woolwich, at the age of sixteen. It was here that he experienced his religious 'conversion'. Kelly alluded to this in his, largely unpublished, autobiography but has left very little account of the event which was to determine the course of his life.

As a result of the conversion experience Kelly left Woolwich and went to Oxford University (Queen's College) in 1879. At Oxford, he recalled later, he learnt two things: 'the width of God's world and of His interest therein [and] the habit of thinking'.[3] It was at Oxford, too, that he discovered the writings of two pioneers of Christian Socialism: Charles Kingsley and Frederick Denison Maurice. The theology of Maurice, in particular, proved to be a significant influence on his theological thinking. Kelly's reading at this time was extensive and catholic, but probably detrimental to his study. He left Oxford with a fourth-class degree in history although, 'I believe I trembled on the edge of a third', he recorded later.[4]

In 1883 Kelly was ordained deacon and served in Kent and then South London. During the next six years he continued to read voraciously: his diary for 1884 lists ninety books. In 1889 Charles Corfe was consecrated as Bishop of Corea [Korea] and looking for missionaries to send there. Kelly approached him with a plan to train men for this role and his offer was accepted. After a brief stay with the Cowley Fathers in Oxford to gain some experience

---

[2] In autobiographical notes written c. 1929–31 Kelly wrote: 'Deafness was a tremendous factor, not because it changed anything, but because it prevented my changing' (SSM/HK/BIO/AB/1).

[3] Every, *No Pious Person*, p. 28.

[4] Quoted in an unpublished typescript by Margaret Dewey, 'SSM Chronicle', in the SSM Archives, p. 20.

of religious life, he moved into 97 Vassall Road, Kennington, on 15 December 1890 and began the Corean Missionary Brotherhood. Most of the men who came were unused to academic study and Kelly was not qualified to provide a theological education; how-ever, the small community did flourish, although few men eventually went to Korea. In 1892 the name was changed to the Society of the Sacred Mission and the scope widened both geographically and theologically.

The Society outgrew Vassall Road and moved to Mildenhall, Suffolk, in 1897 and then to Kelham Hall, Nottinghamshire, in 1903. In 1902 its first overseas mission was established at Modderpoort, South Africa where Herbert Kelly's brother Alfred was installed as the provincial. Kelly was founder and first director of SSM but became increasingly concerned that the 'Society' and 'Herbert Kelly' were being seen as synonymous: 'Kelly & Co.' to quote a later commentator.[5] In 1910 he resigned as director to allow the Society to grow beyond him. In 1925 he explained: 'I do not think "Fr. Founder" a healthy term [...] Only the spade work, the working (or muddling) of purposes was mine. I am not proud of it.'[6]

Kelly's resignation was a great liberation for him and the years 1910–1920 saw him enjoying a freedom and creativity he had not hitherto experienced. He had attended Student Christian Movement (SCM) camps since 1907 and was now able to engage more fully with both SCM and the Ecumenical Movement, first in Edinburgh and Swanwick, and, in 1912, in the USA. His American trip came about at the instigation of the Methodist layman, John R. Mott, founder of the World Student Christian Federation. This experience gave Kelly a life-long interest in ecumenism and led him to write *The Church and Religious Unity*, published in 1913.

---

[5] Edmund Couldrey, Preface to *Great and General Chapters* 1894–1952 (London: SSM Press, 1950). Fr Kelly's Statement to the General Chapter of 1910 is published in this edition.

[6] Kelly, unpublished. 'Appeal to SSM on the relation of SSM to the Church and its authority', p. 7 (SSM/HK/SSM/44).

On return from America, Kelly went east to Japan. He was appointed Professor of Apologetical Theology at the Central Theological College, Ikebukuro. He described these years as his most successful and happiest: 'Japan is "my" country. I spent 5–6 years there, and it is the only bit of my life I can bear to remember. Well, the rest makes me sick and hot (except the Student Movement lot and Swanwick maybe)'.[7]

In 1919 Kelly returned to England. His travels had made him even more critical of what he saw as Kelham's insularity and parochialism however, and he came back to a crisis in the community. For SSM this was a time of post-war reconstruction, and life at Kelham had been disrupted for over four years. His successor as director, David Jenks, had a breakdown in 1919 and was absent from the college. Division had also arisen between the English House and the South African Province over the nature of the religious life and the Anglo-Catholic tradition. At the General Chapter of 1920 there was a bitter debate between the two factions. For Kelly the Chapter of 1920 was 'a misery'.[8] Matters did settle down and Kelly, although he was never completely reconciled to the outcome, took up residence at Kelham under the directorship of Joseph White.

By now he was sixty years old, and his hearing had deteriorated further. Nevertheless, over the next fifteen years he produced his two most successful books, *The Gospel of God*, 1928 and *Catholicity*, 1932. He also refined and developed his scheme of lectures for the College and taught Church History and Dogmatic Theology to the students. At this time he began his correspondence with Dorothy L. Sayers. As these letters show he continued to take an interest in a wide variety of areas from Medieval history and the Inquisition to John Oldham's Oxford Group, the impact of industrialisation and the theology of work. Despite his failing powers, in his last letter to Sayers, three years before his death at the age of ninety, he discussed totalitarianism,

---

[7] Letter 36.
[8] Kelly, *Society of the Sacred Mission Quarterly* [*SSMQ*], 1929.

Aquinas and the Holy Spirit. He concluded: 'I am just so nearly cut off from doing anything now, that I feel a sort of craving to supply *bits of ideas*, such as I have, to people still alive in the world, who can use them'.[9]

Herbert Kelly never featured among the inter-war generation of Anglican 'religious giants' such as J. H. Oldham, Walter Frere, Charles Gore, Neville Talbot or William Temple.[10] Among those who did recognise his significance was Dietrich Bonhoeffer who visited Kelham in 1935, while researching *Life Together*.[11] In an account left of the visit, Kelly is described as:

> The venerable and gifted founder of Kelham, old Father Kelly – sometimes described by the English as a theological precursor of Karl Barth [...] A number of his brilliant lectures were for sale in mimeograph, and we certainly didn't miss the chance [...] I think it was Father Kelly who replied to our question "how do you keep it up?" in the paradoxical words: "I can do it, because I cannot".[12]

Bishop Russell of Southwell in his Foreword to *Gospel of God* wrote:

> In the background always, and sometimes on the platform, was the Eminence Grise, Father Herbert Kelly. Already becoming a legendary figure he was then, as always, *mysterium fascinans* – challenging attention in any context and defying any conventional classification [...] whenever he spoke, and even when he didn't, the spell he wielded was irresistible.

He continued:

> Father Kelly may come into his own again. He would not, perhaps, "go down" with a modern audience. His language, his manner and his idiosyncrasies may date him too much. But he is a prophet for this generation.[13]

---

[9] Letter 44.

[10] See Frank Russell Barry, Bishop of Southwell, in his Foreword to Herbert Kelly, *The Gospel of God* (2nd edition, London: SCM, 1959). This edition was brought out to commemorate the centenary of Kelly's birth.

[11] Dietrich Bonhoeffer, *Life Together*, 1939 (first published in English New York: Harper & Row, 1954).

[12] Julius Rieger in W-D Zimmermann and R. G. Smith: *I Knew Dietrich Bonhoeffer* (New York: Harper & Row, 1966), pp. 97–8.

[13] Frank Russell Barry, Bishop of Southwell, Foreword to Kelly, *The Gospel of God*.

Kelly was an original and creative theologian whose significance was not fully appreciated during his lifetime. Indeed, reading
his considerable output today reveals him to be well ahead of his
time. As Bishop Russell concluded: 'This great man has never been
given his due'. Now is the time.

It is hoped that the letters in this volume will serve as an
introduction to his work and thought for a new generation.

The Correspondents

Herbert Kelly was seventy-seven years old, and living at Kelham
Hall, when the correspondence with Sayers, whom he had never
met, began. His increasing deafness made communication difficult
although he continued to teach until 1945. He also continued to
travel, especially to London where he visited family and friends.

Herbert Kelly in his study at Kelham

He retained his active and enquiring mind until the end. For example, in Letter 22 he described reading and making notes on the Inquisition and 'modern physical theories' as well as returning to an early love in the study of Japanese culture. These letters provide an insight into the mature Kelly's thought and reflections as he looked back over his long life of self-proclaimed 'failure'.

Dorothy L. Sayers, c. 1938

Dorothy Leigh Sayers (1893–1957) was fifty-four at the beginning of the correspondence and at an important moment of her creative life. Brought up in Huntingdonshire where her father, like Kelly's, was a rector, Sayers was academically gifted and went on to gain a first in Modern languages at Oxford (Somerville College) in 1915.[14] After a not altogether successful period of teaching she began work at an advertising agency in London. At this time she had an unhappy relationship with American poet John Cournos and, following their breakup, another romance with Bill White. The affair with White (who, unbeknownst to her at the time, was married) led to the birth of her son, John Antony. Sayers never publicly acknowledged her son but supported him as a nephew, cared for by one of her cousins. In 1926 she married Oswald Arthur 'Mac' Fleming. At the time the correspondence with Kelly began she was an acclaimed detective story writer, best known for her Lord Peter Wimsey mysteries. When Kelly first wrote to her in 1937 she was making the transition from novelist to playwright and, during the course of their correspondence, established herself as a theologian of some note and originality (although 'theologian' was never a term she would apply to herself). At the end of the correspondence (Letter 45) there are references to what would become Sayers' last, and in her view, her most important work; her translation of Dante's *Divine Comedy*.[15] In the letters we see Sayers working out some of her major theological ideas.

The Correspondence

The letters contained in this volume represent the complete extant correspondence between Herbert Kelly and Dorothy L. Sayers, which has never been published in its entirety. The correspon-

---

[14] Although women's degrees were not granted by the University until 1920, and Sayers was one of the first to formally graduate.
[15] Sayers completed the *Inferno* in 1949 and *Purgatorio* in 1955 but died before completion of *Paradiso*. This was finished by her friend and biographer Barbara Reynolds and published in 1962. See: Barbara Reynolds, "Fifty Years On: Dorothy L. Sayers and Dante." *VII: Journal of the Marion E. Wade Center* 16, 1999, pp. 3–6 for an account of Sayers' conception of this project.

dence is kept in the SSM archive collection at the Borthwick Institute, at the University of York, and is composed of original and copied letters.

The copies to complete the set were given by Sayers' son, Antony Fleming in 1982 to Margaret Dewey, librarian at SSM Willen Priory, in 1982. In exchange Dewey sent copies of the SSM side of the correspondence. Fleming was compiling his mother's letters and writings for publication, but died before he was able to finish this work. It was completed by Barbara Reynolds.[16] Fleming's originals are now at the Marion C. Wade Center, Wheaton College, Illinois [MCW]. See Appendices for a list of the letters.

The letters cover ten years of creative growth for Sayers. During this period she wrote her most important theological books and articles. For Herbert Kelly they were years of self-declared 'decline'. He had recently produced *Gospel of God* in 1928 and *Catholicity* in 1932, and continued to develop the ideas he presented in both these volumes over the following ten years. Kelly wrote to Sayers in 1938:

> I can hardly imagine that you have read any books of mine. There are only two going, and neither have attracted any notice (except from the Archbishop of York). One is called the *Gospel of God*, in which I tried to expound just your 'theology'. The other, called *Catholicity* has a final chapter on Confession, where I pressed just your point. N.B. This is another of those matters where, I think, folk want your *explanation* badly.[17]

To read this collection of letters in light of the correspondents' literary output for the period provides a unique insight into the theological inspiration behind their writings. Within the thoughts of these two, apparently very different, personalities with differing backgrounds and life experiences, important theological and philosophical themes connect and are developed. They stimulate

---

[16] Barbara Reynolds, *Dorothy L. Sayers: Her Life and Soul* (New York: St Martin's Press, 1993, revised edition, London, Sceptre Books, 2002). *The Letters of Dorothy L. Sayers*, four volumes, (New York: St Martin's Press, 1996–2000).
[17] Letter 3 and Herbert Kelly, *The Gospel of God*, pp. 147–158.

and seem to inspire each other. In fact there is a convergence in their thought which is encapsulated in Sayers' *The Mind of the Maker*,[18] which Kelly recognises as 'your book, mirrored in my life'.[19]

The correspondence opens with a discussion between Kelly and Sayers of her play *The Zeal of Thy House* [*Zeal*].[20] Her theology of Trinity, of creativity and of the sacrament of work are explored in detail in this early exchange. They discover immediately that they think the same way:

> I'm afraid I haven't read your books, but I will, especially as 'my' theology turns out (and I am very happy to know it) to be 'your' theology also.[21]

Here Kelly is at his most lucid and we see his innovative mind at work. Later his hand-written letters become more discursive and rambling: very much in the manner of a friend thinking aloud. Some of his musings are difficult to follow. As he aged, his writing became indecipherable in places with many crossings out, scribbled insertions and marginal notes. His thoughts seemed to move more quickly than his pen – which never quite caught up. Even within the stream-of-consciousness style of his later letters, however, little gems can be found, for example: 'Medieval papacy is the first instance of a totalitarian state (and the Inquisition the first Gestapo)'.[22]

Sayers herself was to comment on his discursive style:

> Actually, I think I should say that though the style of your writing is easy and familiar, taken sentence by sentence in detail, the presentation of your argument is obscure to the common reader because it leaps very swiftly from point to point without always distinctly showing the connection of ideas. It's rather like the modern kind of music, which passes directly from one unresolved

---

[18] Dorothy L. Sayers, *Mind of the Maker* (first published: 1941, most recent: London: Continuum, 1994).
[19] Letter 37.
[20] All quotations from the play are taken from the most recent published version, Dorothy L. Sayers, *The Zeal of Thy House* (Oregon: Wipf & Stock, 2011).
[21] Letter 4.
[22] Letter 44.

discord to another, leaving the audience to supply the resolution in his head – which is what makes it so baffling to musically ignorant people like me.[23]

Throughout the correspondence both offered constructive and sensitive criticism of each other's work. Sayers' letters were always focussed and tended towards the formal. She responded to Kelly's queries in a considered and detailed manner. We have here a privileged insight into her own thought processes – those of the trained academic mind – and of her humour. At no point did references to her personal life occur, while Kelly frequently introduced family connections, personal reminiscences, and the occasional playful comments: 'Is the new ribbon to celebrate the Garrick? You see I have learnt to notice'.[24]

While Kelly had not read any of Sayer's books when they first began corresponding, he was already a devotee of detective fiction. In two articles in the *Society of the Sacred Mission Quarterly* magazine [*SSMQ*], written just before their correspondence began, he wrote about his discovery of the genre as a way to truth and understanding. After a period of illness he discovered the fiction as a new intellectual pursuit. In Letter 36 he describes it as 'the only moral melodrama left':

> To my mind the ordinary detective doing his proper work, reporting to his proper superiors, is far more interesting than the fancy personalities showing off to their own satisfaction.
> Some writers strive after what one might call 'brighter crime' by mixing in a love story. Sometimes it is a distracted witness who cannot bear that the beautiful girl he has seen should be touched by suspicion [sometimes] it is the detective himself who falls into it. I do not know any instance of more utterly annoying emotionalism.[25]

Given her professional career as an advertising copywriter, as well as detective novelist and reputation as an English scholar, one wonders how Sayers, the creator of Peter Wimsey and Harriet

---

[23] Letter 38.
[24] Letter 20.
[25] *SSMQ*, Christmas, 1935, p. 104.

Vane, would respond to Kelly's concluding comments in the second article:

> One writer remarks that crime stories are the world's worst English. I think that advertisement English is much worse, but you might refuse to call it English at all.[26]

The Drama and the Dogma

Kelly's first letter to Sayers was prompted by his reading of *Zeal*. This play had been commissioned by Canterbury Cathedral for its Festival of Arts and Crafts in 1937 (T. S. Eliot's *Murder in the Cathedral* had been the 1935 production). *Zeal* picked up almost where Eliot left off: four years after the death of Thomas Becket when, in 1170, a fire ravaged the Cathedral. Both events were chronicled by one of the monks, Gervase (who appears in the play).[27] In this, Sayers' first 'religious' play, we see her exploration of key theological themes which she was to revisit in later works. For Sayers, playwriting was a mechanism for transmitting doctrine and making it accessible. It was this which caught Kelly's attention and inspired his first approach to her:

> I wonder if you recognise, or are interested in recognising, how closely your book images the principles of the 'Athanasian Creed' – the twofold necessity of faith in the Trinity of God and the Incarnation.[28]

Sayers responded:

> The neglect of dogma is the curse of nearly all Christian plays, from the playwright's point of view. The dogma of the Incarnation is the

---

[26] *SSMQ*, Easter, 1936, p. 12-13.

[27] See W. Stubbs (ed.), *The Historical Works of Gervase of Canterbury* (London: Longman & Co., 1880) which Sayer's almost certainly drew upon. For general background see Peter Draper, 'Interpretations of the Re-building of Canterbury Cathedral, 1174–1186: Archaeological and Historical Evidence', *Journal of the Society of Architectural Historians*, 56, 1997, pp. 184–203; and Marie-Pierre Gelin, 'Gervase of Canterbury, Christ Church and the Archbishops', *Journal of Ecclesiastical History*, 60, 2009, pp. 449–63.

[28] Letter 1.

most dramatic thing about Christianity, and indeed the most dramatic thing that ever entered into the mind of man.[29]

For her, there is no need for explicit dogma: if the dramatist makes the story accessible enough the teaching will naturally appear.

In *Zeal* Sayers explored her Trinitarian model of Creative Idea (Father), Creative Energy (Son) and Creative Power (Holy Spirit) and articulated it explicitly in Michael's final speech:

> For every work of creation is threefold, an earthly trinity to match the heavenly.
>
> First: there is the Creative Idea; passionless, timeless, beholding the whole work complete at once, the end in the beginning; this is the image of the Father.
>
> Second: there is the Creative Energy, begotten of that Idea, working in time from the beginning to the end, with sweat and passion, being incarnate in the bonds of matter; and this is the image of the Word.
>
> Third: there is the Creative Power, the meaning of work and its response in the lively soul; and this is the image of the indwelling Spirit.
>
> And these three are one, each equally in itself the whole work, whereof none can exist without other; and this is the image of the Trinity.[30]

This concept of an earthly trinity of creativity mirroring the heavenly one is discussed at some length in the correspondence and appears, more fully developed, in Sayers' key work *Mind of the Maker*.[31] In his very first letter Kelly queries the theological basis for her analogical attribution within the Trinity. He makes it clear that any extrapolation from the Augustinian model should place 'idea' as flowing from the Father (or artistic creator) not being the Father (or artistic creator):

> That is St Augustine, but he gives the Trinity as: 'Being, Knowing, Willing'. 1. Being, the reality of an existing mind; 2. The Thought, Word (Logos), or Idea formed in the mind; 3. The Activity, Power,

---

[29] Letter 2.

[30] Sayers, *Zeal*, p.130. This speech was omitted from the first performances at Canterbury but included in the published form, 1937, which Kelly read.

[31] Sayers, *Mind of the Maker*, first published in 1941 (London: Continuum, 1994).

Energy by which the Thought is carried out. You can put it more commonly of things: 1. the thing which is real; 2. the Essence of it, which we seek to know; 3. its activity, what it does, by which we know it.[32]

He goes on:

But in your statements, you have missed out the first and substituted the second – *viz.* the Idea. Then you had to divide the third into Energy (begotten?) and Power. Surely these are the same. It should be: first, there is the living and Eternal God, in Himself infinite, beyond knowledge, unapproachable, but second, revealed in the Creative Idea, in time and in the lively soul.

Sayers 'defends' her analogy by saying she is not drawing on St Augustine but merely presenting:

an effort of my own to make an illustration of three-in-oneness familiar to every creative artist and drawn from his own experience. (The play, by the way, was written to fit in with the Festival of Arts and Crafts at Canterbury, and that it why it is all about craftsmen). St Augustine says that God, in making Man, made an image of the Triune. I am trying to say that Man (made a Craftsman in the image of the Master-Craftsman) in making a work of art presents also an image of the Triune, because every work of creation is threefold.[33]

From a close analysis of the subsequent letters it may be suggested that Kelly was instrumental in Sayers' development of this theology.[34] At the time of their correspondence he too had been exploring very similar ideas of Trinity. In a paper, written in 1937, entitled 'The Will of God and Man', Kelly equated Trinity with Will and identified the three persons of the Trinity as Desire, Intention and Fulfilment.[35] Thus, Desire [Father] conceives a purpose which become Intention [Son] which in turn is brought to Fulfilment [Holy Spirit]. He wrote: 'Between His will and ours the simplest connection is by 'Vocation': God desires and makes his desire known. Man takes God's desire as his own purpose and

[32] Letter 1.
[33] Letter 2.
[34] See Chris Willerton, 'Dorothy L. Sayers and the Creative Reader', *VII: Journal of Marion E. Wade Center*, 28, 2011, pp. 47-60. Herbert Kelly's influence on Sayers has yet to be fully realised by scholars.
[35] 'SSM Vocation', typescript, (SSM/HK/SSM/71).

carries it out (fulfilment)'. Despite some difference in terminology, it is no wonder that they agreed that 'their' theology coincided.

The Creative Idea

The word 'idea' occurs fifty-seven times in the Letters. While some of these references are manners of speech – 'you have no idea' – in the vast majority the word has a special significance which is central to both Kelly's and Sayers' theology. 'Idea', as Kelly articulates it, represents Creativity: God's creativity *in* the world, *in* the incarnation and *through* human work. He used the word to describe his whole life's mission, encapsulated in his first writings: *The History of a Religious Idea* (1898) and *An Idea in the Working* (1908).[36] He sees the connection immediately in Sayers' play: 'first, there is the living and Eternal God, in Himself infinite, beyond knowledge, unapproachable, but second, revealed in the Creative Idea, in time and in the lively soul'.[37] As we have seen above he questions Sayers' placing of the 'idea'. Sayers responds appropriating the powers to human endeavour, recognising the weakness of the human workman in the process: 'William truly observes, "no man's work is perfect" and often the Idea is feeble, the Energy ill-directed and the answer conspicuously lacking'.[38] The Idea is a theme that can be traced through all their letters. For Kelly, as he later acknowledges, it is both his motivating force and his 'failure' in seeing it to fulfilment:

> The Idea was to me quite clear – fifty years ago. Its Incarnation, in the method of teaching and in the lectures was reasonably good (anyhow in the History was). The Power, well about the results, I am utterly at sea. This side is always my weakness. I am never effective – not as a teacher or otherwise.[39]

---

[36] Both published at Kelham (SSM Press).
[37] Letter 1.
[38] Letter 2.
[39] Letter 37.

The chapters in Sayers' book *Mind of the Maker* on 'Idea, Energy and Power', and 'The Energy Revealed in Creation' are a direct development of much that is discussed in this correspondence.

Spiritual or Religious?

Another area in which the two held similar views was their understanding of a living faith in an incarnate God. Both Kelly and Sayers witnessed in the post-World War One years a 'pleading of despair': a spiritual emptiness that seemed not to be served by traditional Christian churches.[40] They deplored the growth of 'nice', 'spiritual' feelings as a substitute for real, living engagement with the God of Truth. While differing in how large a part the intellect should play in faith, both recognised that a good understanding of doctrine was essential to maintaining Christianity – and that doctrine did not sit comfortably in modern 'spirituality'. God was fine, in his place: 'People want God – but up in heaven, out of the way'[41] wrote Kelly, not a God who challenged comfortable, contemporary *mores*. Moreover, if they did accept Jesus (and the letters contain discussion on the Incarnation and the human/divine person of Jesus) this could be equally damaging:

> "Gentle-Jesus-meek-and-mild" has probably made more apostates than any other single phrase in the language. And what a phrase! About as adequate as calling a man-eating tiger "poor pussy"!'[42]

Sayers took up this theme again later:

> I believe it to be a grave mistake to present Christianity as something charming and popular with no offence in it. [...] We cannot blink the fact that gentle Jesus meek and mild was so stiff in His opinions and so inflammatory in His language that He was thrown out of

---

[40] Kelly, *Gospel of God*, p.136.
[41] Letter 3.
[42] Letter 4.

church, stoned, hunted […] and finally gibbeted as a firebrand and a public danger.[43]

Her purpose in *Zeal* was to make Christianity real and relevant: 'People come away from it with the idea that religion is interesting and exciting and practical, and not just a kind of dreary and sloppy emotion about something that has nothing to do with life'.[44] This inspired Kelly to write:

> How wonderful and delightful a thing it is to me to find a writer of your influence who […] can state the vital force of a Christian faith in God and His Christ, not in the abstract fashion which is all we theologians can reach, but in a living pictorial fashion which common people can follow […] I do not remember to have seen any "popular" (as opposed to a definitely religious book), which has ever seen the possibility of a "theological" faith as the true explanation of our life.[45]

Sayers' aim was to combine dogma and drama, although she would never allow the drama to be sacrificed for dogma. As she wrote to her friend Dorothy Rowe in 1937:

> If one has to write a play on a religious subject, the only way to do it is to avoid wistful emotionalism and get as much drama as one can out of sheer hard dogma. After all, nothing can be more essentially dramatic than Catholic doctrine; but all is lost if one surrounds it with a vague cloud of let-us-all-feel-good-and-loving-and-God-won't-mind-anything-much.[46]

In this approach she struck an immediate chord for Kelly whose teaching had asserted that an emotive and vague 'spirituality' was not the way forward. As long back as 1906, in a circular letter to his brethren at SSM, *Ad Fratres*, he had discussed the current theological situation and written:

> The real and central hinge of all hope of a religious regeneration, I believe, lies in substituting faith as the dominant religious motive instead of feeling; and, for its object, the actual power of God in the place of "piety": the delight of learning, beholding, obeying […] for

---

[43] Sayers, 'Creed or Chaos?' in the essay collection *Creed or Chaos?* first published in 1947. (Manchester: NH, Sophia Institute Press, 1974), p. 22.
[44] Letter 2.
[45] Letter 1.
[46] Reynolds, *The Letters of Dorothy L. Sayers*, volume II, pp. 22–23.

the mere enjoyment and possession of a comfortable sentiment within one's own individuality.[47]

Michael Ramsey, writing on Herbert Kelly's 'Educational Method and Dogma' has summed up what in essence 'Fr. Kelly went on saying again and again and again':

> Let me quote to you some remarks he made from time to time which he made at the SCM conferences at Swanwick. "What does God do? Does God do anything, or is God only a name for our ideals?" "There used to be a thing called theology; it was about God. Now we have a thing called psychology of religion, and it's all about your own nice feelings." That is Kelly in a nutshell. Of course, it raises questions as well as answering them, but no harm in that: The weight of his influence was this distinction between the living God and man's thoughts about him, man's feeling derived from him. Thus to Fr. Kelly dogma mattered enormously, but not as something to be idolized as a kind of utterly rigid system, because dogma is merely a necessary but inadequate witness to the living God.[48]

The similarity with Dorothy L. Sayers' approach is marked:

> It is a lie to say dogma does not matter: it matters enormously. It is fatal to let people suppose that Christianity is only a mode of feeling; it is vitally necessary to insist that it is first and foremost a rational explanation for the universe.[49]

This is another belief that Kelly had asserted 'again and again'. In a Newsletter of 1911 he described, in his unconventional style, a talk he had given on 'Faith and Authority' to a meeting at the Student Christian Movement camp that year:

> I jammed in the difference between belief, which is of opinion, i.e. of static proposition, and faith or belief *in*, which is of facts. All sensible belief rests upon reason, which must be your own reason. But though it is because of reason, it is not *in* reason, but in a *thing*. I believe that the rope is sound through syllogisms starting from a red worsted thread (Alpine Club mark), but it is the rope itself that takes my weight, manila hemp, not syllogisms nor worsted. [...] Authority is the experience of unnumbered common men as

---

[47] Herbert Kelly, *Ad Fratres*, 1906.
[48] Part of a talk given by Michael Ramsey, as archbishop of York in 1960 on the anniversary of Kelly's birth. Reproduced in *SSMQ: H.K. Centenary edition*, September 1960, pp. 46–51.
[49] Sayers, *Creed or Chaos?* p.22.

opposed to clever people [...] Then on the Creeds. They have nothing to do with opinions, but a belief *in*. They attempted only to make clear what was the meaning of that "thing" in which we trusted, what we trusted it for. Lastly on faith as salvation, i.e. getting away from self. It wasn't over well done, but they liked it enormously. Partly, as usual, because they had never heard theology talked with an easy, unconventional slang: I explained to 'em that it wasn't slang, and I would not have it so called; it was *koine*. Made my reputation for that camp.[50]

The Creed had always been central to Kelly's teaching. In an unpublished paper, 'Personal Thoughts Concerning Unity', written in 1926, he recalled that: 'It was about 1900 that [...] I had to get down seriously to St Augustine and his Predestinarianism'.[51] And this led him to make the drama of the Creed form the basis of his dogmatics courses, indeed of all Kelham education:

The Creed is in three parts – (a) What is God? What is an Infinite Will? There cannot be a world-order except around that Will. But how can man come to it? It is plain he cannot, but (b) there is a Gospel telling us that God came to man, and took his World-Order to Himself, redeemed it – not, as we always think, by "what He does," but by what He suffered – and out of that made Triumph and Ascension. (c) But in as much as we are separate beings with independent wills, choices, judgements, what we have we, or can we have, in a common Redemption? How is this Infinite Will, Eternal and Universal, related to the individual will?[52]

To stray from creedal belief, he believed, was fatal for humanity:

Whenever people lose their faith in God, and begin to think about themselves, they are always silly. But it is very pathetic and very dangerous all the same [...]
There is generally no better way, there is often no other way, of getting back to faith in God than by finding out suddenly what we are without Him.[53]

In describing 'The Kelham Course' in the *SSMQ* in the 1930s Kelly wrote:

[50] *SSMQ* 1911.
[51] SSM/HK/UPW/29, 1926.
[52] Ibid, some parts of this paper are reproduced in Dewey, 'SSM Chronicle', pp. 37ff.
[53] Kelly, *An Idea in the Working* (Kelham: SSM Press,1967), p. 66–7.

The Catholic Creeds start from one positive assertion: "I believe in one God"; the rest is an explanation, either of the meaning, or of the road to, that amazing statement – first, as thus: in one God, i.e. the Father, the Son, and the Holy Ghost. The "Athanasian" statement gives the worship of the Trinity as the primary substance of the "Catholic Faith." Fr. Benson maintained that "the decadence of Christendom began when the Middle Ages shup up that doctrine in Latin treaties for the clergy." We all realise that the Trinity is the key and centre of all faith in a real and living God. It is not given to us a fresh perplexity and a trial of "faith"; but, as the key of our life, we must learn to use it. It seems difficult, just because that reality is so frightening. Once in Eden (Gen. iii), as afterwards in Gethsemane, men met the "voice" of God, and did not at all like it.[54]

For Kelly this amazing fact needed to be proclaimed continually to an ignorant world. As Sayers observed, in Letter 2, 'It does seem just as well, if you are going to disbelieve a thing, to find out exactly what you are disbelieving'.[55]

Vocation: Work, Creativity and Faith

The relationship between human creativity and God's work in creation is, as we saw above, a central theme in both *Zeal* and these letters. Sayers wrote at length about the integrity of the crafts-person's work and the problem of the artist who neglects God for that work. One must always aim for the highest possible standard but ultimately the worker must see his or her own place within the Creator's work. The fundamental sin of Sayers' hero William is not his illicit affair with Lady Ursula but his pride. He can only redeem this personal weakness when he acknowledges his work solely as a tribute to the Divine Creator:

Let me lie deep in hell,
Death gnaw upon me, purge my bones with fire,
But let my work, all that was good in me,

---

[54] *SSMQ*, Michaelmas and Christmas 1937 and Easter 1938. See also Dewey, 'SSM Chronicle' p. 182.
[55] Letter 2.

All that was God, stand up and live and grow.[56]

Margaret Wiedemann Hunt has observed: 'Sayers believed that the dramatic experience was itself one in which writers, actors and audiences were united in a God-given and God-like creative process'.[57] Indeed, Sayers may be seen as suggesting in some of these letters that the theatre could provide what the church was no longer supplying and, in fact take its place in evangelisation. She certainly complained that:

> [...] the Church [has] lost Her hold on reality [...] in Her failure to understand and respect the secular vocation. She has allowed work and religion to become separate departments, and is astonished to find that, as a result, the secular work of the world is turned to purely selfish and destructive ends.[58]

Rather than exhorting the 'intelligent carpenter' against drink and immorality the Church should be telling him that 'the very first demand that his religion makes upon him is that he should make good tables'.[59] Sayers shares with Kelly her emerging idea of the need for a Christian doctrine of work in Letter 35. Unfortunately, Kelly does not respond directly to this here and one suspects his views differed (see Letter 37). He was never afraid to disagree with her and he commented later on her discussion of Christ's role in work: '[I] don't like you saying, "Christ resolutely refused to sit on committees" (He wasn't asked) or to "argue about politics" (He never argued about anything)'.[60]

The Kelly-Sayers letters may be seen by scholars as a link in the chain of Sayers' working out of her theology of the sacrament of creative work. From the tentative first steps in the novel *Gaudy Night* (1935) to full expression in *Mind of the Maker* (1941) and *Creed and Chaos?* (1947), the working out can be discerned in the

[56] Sayers, *Zeal of Thy House*, Act IV, p. 126.
[57] Margaret Wiedemann Hunt, 'Playwrights are not Evangelists: Dorothy L. Sayers on Translating the Gospels into Drama', *Studies in Church History*, 53, 2017, pp. 405–19.
[58] Dorothy L. Sayers, 'Why Work', 1942, *Creed or Chaos?* pp. 63–84.
[59] Ibid, pp. 76–77.
[60] Letter 35.

intervening correspondence. For Sayers, it is better for the Church that a great work is produced by a non-believer than a mediocre work by an avowed Christian. If Kelly went on to read *Gaudy Night* he would have discovered that the theme of *Zeal,* in embryonic form, is there.[61] It seemed to Sayers 'obvious that the theme of *Gaudy Night* and *Zeal* were fundamentally one and the same: the overriding importance of work itself, be it the pursuit of academic truth or the building of a cathedral'.[62] Kelly did not altogether agree with this; for him the intention or purpose behind the work was also of importance. He deals with this in *Gospel of God*: 'The purpose may not be high enough, or perhaps the vision is not clear enough, greatly to exalt his life, yet there is enough to keep his life straight'.[63] To seek God and to try to glorify him in all one does is more important to Kelly than the publicly perceived outcome.

Theology of Work and Individualism

Creativity, work, intention and vocation are themes that run through the correspondence. In 1941 Kelly and Sayers were discussing work and education, especially of 'the masses'. Sayers had given a talk in March of that year on 'Work and Vocation'.[64] Kelly too was working on a theology of work which was published that same year in an article, 'Industrialism and the Individual'.[65] In their respective papers both discuss that work can be: 'itself a sacrament and manifestation of man's creative energy' and deplored the fact that 'the workers' are not aware of their link in the chain of production in order to have 'a more vivid sense of their usefulness'.[66]

---

[61] In 1940 he confessed: 'Re. Detective stories. I hardly read anything else now (bein' 80)', Letter 36.

[62] Reynolds, *Dorothy L. Sayers: Her Life and Her Soul*, p. 322.

[63] Kelly, *Gospel of God*, p. 51.

[64] Later published as 'Why Work?' in *Creed or Chaos?* pp. 63–84.

[65] *SSMQ* Easter, 1941.

[66] Herbert Kelly, 'Industrialism and the Individual', *SSMQ* Easter 1941, p. 6–7.

In a series of essays produced during the early 1940s Sayers decried what she saw as an 'unsacramental attitude' to work which was, tacitly at least, upheld by the Church.

> From the eighteenth century onwards [the Church] has tended to acquiesce in what I may call the "industrious apprentice" view of the matter: "Work hard and be thrifty and God will bless you with a contented mind and a competence". This is nothing but enlightened self-interest in its vulgarist form and plays directly into the hands of the monopolist and financier.[67]

In 'Why Work?' she wrote that the Church had forgotten that 'the secular vocation is sacred. Forgotten that a building must be good architecture before it can be a good church' and went on to describe the Christian doctrine of work as 'very closely related to the doctrines of creative energy of God and the divine image in man.'[68]

The modern tendency to equate work with gainful employment she viewed as fundamentally heretical. Some of her proposals here are very *ad rem* to our present era. For example: If a human being's fulfilment of their true nature is to be found in a full expression of their divine creativeness then a Christian doctrine of work must be embraced which provides: 'not only for proper conditions of employment, but also that the work shall be such as a man may do with his whole heart, and that he shall do it for the work's sake'. She recognised how hard it is to accept this sacramental attitude to work while, 'many people are forced, by our evil standard of values, to do work which is spiritual degeneration – a long series of financial trickeries for example – or the manufacture of vulgar and useless trivialities'. However, even in the more class conscious 1940s some of her comments still appeared elitist and unsympathetic to the 'common man'.[69]

In Letter 37 Kelly challenged Sayers on her discussion of industrialisation and unemployment and suggested: 'MM [Middleton

---

[67] Sayers, 'Why Work', 1942, see *Creed or Chaos?* pp. 63–84.
[68] Ibid, pp. 77–8.
[69] Sayers, *Mind of the Maker*, p. 179.

Murry] seems to me to be grousing at common folks as God makes them'. He returned to this gentle criticism in his next letter:

> May I risk myself – as a priest – if I say don't be *bitter* over common folk? You've had a lot – "addressing people and arguing" with very common and stupid people – who are frightened of you (e.g. Baptists in *British Weekly*). Thank God, He lets you do it and that they will listen, they won't [to] me. It is awful hard to get people to see what they have never seen. After all, if God has made stupid people, we must be sympathetic over them – I take it He is.[70]

In this he has a point which will strike the modern reader more perhaps than it did his contemporaries. Although the frequent accusations of Sayers' intellectual and social snobbery are not without foundation, her position is more nuanced. To write that 'the common man' is less likely to take pride in his work than the artist and identify that: 'what distinguishes [the artist] from the man who works to live is, I think, his desire to see the fulfilment of his work' is certainly galling in today's world of zero-hours contracts and financial instability, but if we all had a 'right attitude' to work and awareness of the impact of the final product we may, perhaps, be able to review the concept of labour. Some of Sayers' comments are pertinent to today's discussions on equality, fair wages, and ethical and unethical trading.

In comparing Kelly's writing in the 1940s with Sayers' various offerings, however, his approach seems generally more realistic, compassionate and attuned with twenty-first century values. Possibly this is because he related more readily to 'the simple man':

> Great work is done by great minds reaching out. Commonplace folk, intellectually "poor", can only pick up crumbs. "Cheap knowledge"? Please, it is all I have, but may I not give thanks to God, who takes thought even on the sparrows? When we give thanks before a meal, do not forget the cooking – and the gas workers.[71]

Kelly had long identified the centrality of work in a person's life – but also the danger thereof. In *An Idea in the Working*, he observed in connection with the Kelham life:

---

[70] Letter 39.
[71] Kelly, 'Structure of the Modern Age', *SSMQ*, Easter, 1948, p. 4.

Yet it is far easier for a man to accept these requirements [of poverty and celibacy] than it is for him to give up his own work, to regard it as a part of a common work, to make his own ideas and plans part of a common plan. Comfort and family are after all external, and he can abstain from them, but he cannot abstain from his work. The more earnest, the more devoted he is to it, the more absorbed he will be in it, and the more his work becomes his real self. Then the freedom of movement is lost. Love for one's work is sometimes a very subtle form of self-love; it is in any case a great tie.[72]

In 1941 he discussed the role of the individual in the mass machinery of industrialism in all its forms and asked: 'What can we do with this individuality called the Self?' He recognised that the majority of us will never know where we 'fit' in God's great work of redemption any more than the munition workers in the factory. He asked:

What if our part does not fit in? That hurts, and badly. It is part of being crucified. Some say we ought not to mind apparent failure. I think that inhuman, but we must put up with it. Success or failure, joy or pain, do not think more than you have to of your own share. By us, or perhaps by others, God's purpose goes on, and one day we shall see His glory, which is *in eius voluntate*, in the fulfilment of His will.[73]

In this context his earlier comments that the search for self was replacing the search for God seem remarkably prescient: 'how deeply the spirit of individualism, the desire to do things for oneself, in one's own way and at one's own choice, had taken hold of the English mind', he stated then.[74] Forty years later, in summing up the motto of SSM, *Ad Gloriam Dei in eius voluntates*, he posited a possible answer:

What then *ought* to be our individual relation to a whole purpose? [...] [the] plain and certain truth that God's cause and God's glory alone matter. In consequence, to think of your own place or success is to lose direction.[75]

---

[72] Kelly, *An Idea in the Working*, p. 29.
[73] Kelly, 'Industrialism and the Individual', *SSMQ* Easter 1941, pp. 6–7.
[74] Kelly, *An Idea in the Working*, p. 99.
[75] Kelly, 'Industrialism and the Individual', p. 6.

And here we can discern a theology of self in Kelly's writing: it is a concept of the true self – which can only be found through humility and total renunciation. In a talk to students at Swanwick in 1927 he summed up this approach in an address 'God, His World and the Self'.

> Facing life, you ask what am I going to do. It is a good question, but the most real question is "What is God going to do with you?" And it is no use throwing that question back at me. I have no more idea what the answer is than you have. It lies between you and God [...]
>
> Here is the dialogue of the soul with God. You are only one of all mankind crying in the dark, as I imagine it, "Lord, why have you made me thus?"
>
> And the answer given to all –"Beloved, I made you for myself".
>
> "But why am I in the dark and in confusion?"
>
> "Beloved, you are in the dark and in confusion because you are seeking for light and wisdom in yourself. You will not find them there".
>
> "But why cannot I know what you are doing?"
>
> "Because that is part of a whole universe of meaning, and you cannot know universes. You want to be a God, a lord of the world, when you are only a little self".
>
> [...] don't be afraid of being silly and rather absurd. You and I are only God's little children. Only don't pretend you aren't. Learn to laugh – laugh especially at yourself. If we could hear the angels chuckling over our solemnity, we might learn a lot, but they are very nice and don't want to hurt our feelings, so they keep it to themselves. Children are very solemn and very easily discouraged. So are we.
>
> "Fight for what God has given you, but never for a personal question. Your position, your importance, what people think of you, does not help, it only obscures, the issue".[76]

Responding to Sayers' call for a doctrine of work (Letter 35) Kelly articulated the need for a doctrine of the Holy Spirit (Letter 36), this difference in emphasis (from creating to allowing oneself to be created) suggests that, though their theology was 'the same', their approach to it sometimes differed.

---

[76] Reprinted in *SSMQ*, Michaelmas 1927. See also Dewey, 'SSM Chronicle' p. 147.

Roman/Anglican Catholics

To modern readers the anti-Roman Catholic polemic in the letters may feel uncomfortable. But the 'threat' of Rome was very real to many Anglicans at this time. The crisis at Kelham following World War I centred around 'Romanising tendencies' with several members leaving to be received into the Roman Catholic Church. The common view was that Roman Catholicism was anti-intellectual and emotional: for Kelly, Roman Catholics (as represented by the 'Romanisers' at Kelham) were unreflective, dogmatic and 'It is their infallibilism and violence [...] and above all their contempt for reasonableness and thought which alienates me'.[77] Kelly, it can be argued, was 'catholic' in the broadest and least partisan sense of the word and for him the Anglican Church was catholic. This is what he argued all his life, particularly in *SSMQ* papers such as 'Anglicanism' and his book *Catholicity*.[78] He was concerned with reconciling the Catholic and Evangelical parties within the Church of England. Arguing that historic schisms and differences should be treated as just that, historic. That history informs our understanding and development but it is unreasonable to base our present claims completely on them – 'any more than it would be reasonable to base a modern claim on the intellectual services of Athens and Alexandria'.[79] This, he saw, as the 'problem' with Rome who had 'brought herself into a position in which she was incapable of adapting herself to any new fashion of thinking'.[80] This does not mean that Kelly was 'anti-Roman Catholic' *per se*, but he was alive to the dangers he saw it as posing to the Catholic wing of his church and was not above some sweepingly negative statements on the subject. His family background was Evangelical and it was only after ordination that his position began to change:

---

[77] Letter to David Jenks, undated (SSM/HK/C/L/7).
[78] Kelly, 'Anglicanism', *SSMQ* Christmas 1932, pp. 90–7; Kelly, *Catholicity* (London: SCM, 1932).
[79] 'Anglicanism', p. 90.
[80] Ibid, p. 94.

It was during those parish years that I became definitely "Catholic." I knew no one worth knowing in Catholic circles, and the few I did know were not very helpful, since to them "the authority of the Church" was always apt to mean a series of doctrines stated by a recognised authority. The idea of a Catholic Church and of Catholic authority made an immense appeal to me. It was a vision of a great, whole, ordered, common Truth – wherein men at all times lived. One God, One faith. Protestantism, with its talk of private judgement, ceased to appeal to me. That I am a little private individual, making my own way, is a fact, but it is not a basis of faith. My faith lies beyond myself – in a Universal Truth which is God's Spirit. Certainly the phrase "Scripture as interpreted by Catholic consent" seemed to come as near the truth as any phrase can. I would never separate myself from that consent, but Pusey's apparent belief that the teaching of God's Spirit could be fixed by a catena of consensual extracts, seemed to me to break down in fact as it does in principle. I could never be a Roman, because that theory is a formal substitution (vicariate) of another process for the living God. I am a learner. I wanted to learn from an eternal Spirit of all ages – primitive, mediaeval, modern – the self-same Spirit.[81]

In a letter written to an unnamed recipient at the very end of his life Kelly appears to be answering the question why he is 'anti-Catholic'. The letter is in his usual muddled and discursive style, but he seems to be drawing on Church history to equate the totalitarianism of the Roman Church with that of twentieth-century communism. He writes: 'You speak of being "Anti-Roman". There is a reason for it – I am prejudiced against any totalitarianism'.[82] Many years earlier Kelly had written in a similar, though more coherent, vein to a friend in Japan whom he feared was being drawn into the Roman Church. He wrote distinguishing between Roman Catholicism and 'true Catholicity', as he saw it:

The Romans say "There is one Church. It must all be in obedience to the Bishop of Rome". We say that is not catholic. The Church in England is the Catholic Church in England, and the Church in Japan is the Catholic Church of Japan. If the Church of England tried to make the Japanese Church just like the English Church, that would be very foolish […] It would be very unchristian. I do not want you

[81] Kelly, 'Personal Thoughts Concerning Unity' (SSM/HK/UPW/29 1927 and quoted in Dewey, 'SSM Chronicle' p. 21).
[82] Letter 27 March 1949 (SSM/HK/C/L/836).

to be a Roman Catholic nor an English Catholic. I want your Church to be Nippon sei Kokwai. I do not believe in the Bishop of Rome, because I believe in God.[83]

For Sayers too, her view of Roman Catholicism was coloured by her experiences, background and culture as well as understanding of the dogmas of faith. She too was aware of the dangers posed by what a character in one her novels describes as 'Roaming Catholics'.[84] The rumour that she herself was to 'go over to Rome', reported in Letter 21, she rebuffed with some force in Letter 22.

Both Kelly and Sayers believed in ecumenism. In their writing they focused on what Sayers called 'an Oecumenical Doctrine'; a theology which was acceptable to 'the three Catholic branches of the Churches: Roman, Greek Orthodox and Anglican'.[85] For Kelly this had begun with the Student Christian Movement in the early 1900s and at the First World Missionary Conference in 1910. This, originally very Evangelical Protestant body:

> sought to reach out into the Anglo-Catholic, the Eastern Orthodox, and the Roman Catholic worlds, for the Lord prayed that they all might be one. As early as the years when "Edinburgh 1910" was being prepared, the ecumenical task was seen in these inclusive terms, and this was because the problem had already been faced in the British Student Christian Movement and a solution found in what was called the "inter-denominational position." That the British SCM had developed this position at all is largely due to the influence within it of Herbert Kelly and Neville Talbot.[86]

The language used in these letters must be understood in the context of the times in which they were written. Anglican-Roman Catholic relations continued to be influenced by historical prejudice and mistrust on both sides, which only began to change with the Second Vatican Council in the 1960s.[87]

---

[83] Letter to Mago Keiichi, 28 October 1921 (SSM/HK/C/L/61).
[84] Dorothy L. Sayers, *Unnatural Death*, Chapter 19, 1927.
[85] Sayers, Letter to Rev. Neville Gorton, 24 September 1941, Reynolds, *Letters*, *Vol II*, pp. 297–300. See also Kathryn Wehr, 'Disambiguation: Sayers as a Catholic' in *VII Journal of the Marion E. Wade Center*, 33, 2016, pp. 7–18.
[86] David M. Paton, Introduction, Every (ed.), *No Pious Person*, p. 8.
[87] SSM was in the vanguard here, especially in the work of Fr Gabriel Hebert, who was involved, among other activities in the Conference between Anglicans

Kelham Pedagogy

'My business is education' wrote Kelly in Letter 37. He had indeed been an educator since 1890 and the focus of his educational programme had always been the 'ninety per cent of average chaps'. This is enshrined in the SSM Constitution, which states the principal aim of the Society as being the 'training those of whom at present use cannot be made or is not made, whether through their lack of means or of education, or through other causes'.[88] Unlike other Anglican communities such as the Cowley Fathers or Community of the Resurrection, SSM had always drawn the majority of its recruits from the lower middle or working class, who had often received no more than an elementary education. Early members of the Society included carpenters, shop assistants, clerks, printers, teachers and journalists.

In Letter 37 Kelly sets out his agenda for Kelham:

> [...] they [university dons] think exclusively of the ten per cent of clever chaps. They do not understand or care for the other ninety per cent. I do not say they are wrong. Maybe that is university business, but it is not the theological college business.

It certainly was not Kelham business which, from the outset, had been insistent that men training for the ministry need not be graduates.[89] One of his many battles with the Church hierarchy was against the 1917 ruling of Bishops that all ordinands must have degrees. Kelly believed that theological education must be concerned with a holistic cultural teaching. 'Theology is a view of life as a whole and universities are less and less accustomed to wholes', he wrote in 1919.[90] For this reason too, manual work was always an important part of the training at Kelham: meditation,

---

and Roman Catholics at Worth Abbey in 1962 ('Dialogue at Worth', SSM/GH/EC/15).

[88] SSM Constitution, 1893.

[89] For a detailed explanation of his views see: Kelly, *The Universities and Training for the Clergy* (London: Sherratt & Hughes, 1909).

[90] Herbert Kelly, 'The Training and Examination of Candidates for Orders', *Church Quarterly Review*, 1919, p. 358.

prayer, worship, scrubbing stairs and washing dishes were all essential components of the programme.

> Theology I conceive to be the study of the vision, of the great life-purpose, and there is no ultimate purpose except God. If our theology is unpractical, it is that view of life-purpose that we have missed. It is possible that we have missed "theology" and are only studying "theological subjects".[91]

In 1903, Kelly set out his pedagogical approach in a pamphlet, *On the Aim and Methods of Theological Study,* which he addressed to students outlining the purpose and philosophy of theological study, the subjects to be covered and the methods of thinking and writing.[92] For Kelly knowledge of God (and of self) were the only aims of theological training. God and theological education were inextricably linked.

Kelham theology, *Kelly's* theology, was 'not a technical and professional knowledge':

> We were studying God's view of human life, what God was doing on the Somme, and at Westminster and at Tilbury Docks. [...] I do not want to know what you can do with Christ in a church (building) half as much as I want to know what Christ is doing in the street.[93]

And here we touch on another Kelly theme which is apparent in the Letters: his despair at the restriction of God in church services and lack of good teaching from the pulpit. For him the point is always God, not religion. His goal at Kelham was to teach a different way of preaching and of living:

> A young ordinand got talking with one of my boys and said: "The worst of your view is that it would bring God into everything". Terrible that. People want God – but up in heaven, out of the way. I call it the "externality of God".[94]

It was not that Kelly didn't believe that you couldn't, shouldn't, seek God first in a formal setting of church or chapel

---

[91] Kelly, 'Personal Thoughts Concerning Unity' (1926), SSM/HK/UP/29.
[92] Herbert Kelly, *On the Aim and Methods of Theological Study* (Kelham: SSM Press, 1903).
[93] Kelly, *Ad Filios*, 1920.
[94] Letter 3.

but he is forceful on the common notion of being 'spiritual but not religious': 'I can pray in a field better than in church':

> We were well aware that you must find Christ in the church before you will find Him anywhere else (on the football field) but the two are not the same. It is quite possible to find Him in church and never think of looking for Him anywhere else. The worship of the parish church is the key which should unlock the mystery of God in the world. Is it not being very generally used to lock the mystery up – safely within the church itself?[95]

The mature Kelly, reflecting on his life, sees his teaching and the college as his main aim, his 'idea', in life:

> God has taken away all, except this: teaching these boys. I was trying to teach them not to learn up History, but to understand men's minds – what God was doing – what they thought they were doing and what they missed. And not to learn correct doctrine with appropriate arguments, but to think them and see in them a Gospel to life, to science and to thought.[96]

This is Kelly's pedagogy in a nutshell.

A Theology of Failure

There is a suggestion of perfectionism, possibly almost Pelagianism, in some of Sayers' messages that did not sit easily with Kelly, whose theology may be summed up as one of failure.[97] For him the emphasis was less on the material results – the most beautifully constructed cathedral or perfectly crafted poem – than on the intention and faith behind the striving and mess of life:

> I took a dear old Father to see some "proofs of the being of God" – actually I called them "proofs of the resurrection." I showed him our fat old pigs, screamingly ugly, placidly self-satisfied. Oh yes! If I had showed you flowers, and sunsets, and stars, you would have said. "Ah! How true!" But I do not feel as if I greatly wanted God to tell

---

[95] Kelly, *Ad Filios*.
[96] Letter 37.
[97] This has been explored by Alan Williams Jones in his, unpublished, PhD thesis 'Herbert Hamilton Kelly S.S.M. 1860–1950: A Study in Failure', University of Nottingham, 1971 (SSM/TH/1).

me that beautiful things are beautiful. I desperately want to know if
there is a God who understands that bundle of incompetence and
commonplace, ugliness and self-satisfaction, which make the most
obvious experiences of that sublime thing I call my Personality. Can
he make any use or sense of it?[98]

Sayers in all her writings stressed that the best way to serve God
was to fulfil one's natural talent – 'if your natural talent is for
barbering, wouldn't it be better to *be* a barber, and a good barber
[…]'.[99] But what if you believe you have no talent? In Letter 37
Kelly applied her theory to himself and ruminated on his
ambitions and failures, 'Once I fancied myself as a preacher […] it
became evident to me that no one else did […] I did think I might
write something. They [his books] never took on'.[100]

In a paper sent to the Anglican Benedictine monk and lit-
urgical scholar, Gregory Dix, Kelly stated this view more baldly:

It is only necessary to say: "All that is good (nice) in me is of grace",
yet the real perplexities of life come here: concerning the fashioning
of our work and the upshot of it. God gives you and me a heap of
things to do, big and little […] then a life work – maybe a shop,
maybe some vast idea […] and they are *all* His to be done in His
way. It hits me badly. I have had ideas, theological and practical, ever
so big.

I have tried writing books, lecturing, preaching, and have never
really brought anything off. It is just blundering incapacity which
wrecks and seems to mark everything.[101]

Sayers' response to this would have been interesting.

In Letters 36, 37 and 39 Kelly provides a kind of retrospective
of his life and sums up his present state as 'old, tired, spent,
disappointed, very jealous […]'.[102] He writes in a similar vein, and
even more candidly, to Gregory Dix that same year:

---

[98] From an address to the SCM 'Camp II', *SSMQ* Michaelmas 1927 (SSM/S/6).
[99] Sayers, *Gaudy Night* (London, Gollanz, 1935), p. 47.
[100] Letter 37.
[101] HK/C/L/815/2 (c.1943). Regarding preaching his experience was, from the
outset, a 'failure': 'At first, I preached occasionally, but they petitioned that the
curate should not preach'. From the unpublished autobiography,
SSM/HK/BIO/AB/1, see also Dewey, 'SSM Chronicle', p. 21
[102] Letter 39.

I can, and do, lie awake and scream over the fool things I did; not sins – as Chesterton said (before his apostacy): "you can get absolution for murdering your grandmother – not for spilling the soup" [...] I have tried writing books, lecturing, preaching, and have never really brought anything off. It is just blundering, incapacity which wrecks – and seems to mark – everything.[103]

The years he spent in Japan (1913–1919) were among the happiest of his life. It is significant that these, and the other initiatives he lists as being 'successes' (involvement in SCM and the Ecumenical Movement), all happened after his retirement as director of SSM and when he was away from Kelham. He was ever a maverick and didn't fit anywhere easily, not even in the Order he had founded.

Herbert Kelly comes across in some of these letters as an eccentric figure: 'the old man' as he was fondly referred to at Kelham, who had become a legend even in his lifetime: a *'mysterium fascinans'*.[104] But we also get many glimpses of the originality and creativity of his thought. Dorothy L. Sayers too, in her personal life and writings, presents a series of contradictions. Here we see her at a developmental moment in her career and faith, and Kelly is revealed as having had an important role in this development, if only as a sounding board. Sayers is recognised as an important apologetic voice in twentieth-century Christian literature and Kelly as an *eminence grise* in twentieth-century Anglican theology.[105] These letters reveal them both to be worthy of rediscovery in the twenty-first century.

---

103 HK to Gregory Dix, 1944 (HK/C/L/815/2).
104 Southwell, Foreword to *The Gospel of God*, p.7.
105 Ibid.

THE LETTERS

1 October 1937

Dear Miss Sayers,

I am merely a theological tutor in a theological college – as above. I read your *Zeal of Thy House*, and I had a longing to tell you how wonderful and delightful a thing it is to me to find a writer of your influence who actually realises and can state the vital force of a Christian faith in God and His Christ, not in the abstract fashion which is all we theologians can reach, but in a living pictorial fashion which common people can follow. There are books which refer to 'religion', generally on its moral side; occasionally, though rarely, with sympathy; most often with a patronising indifference; quite often with bitter scorn and dislike. I do not remember to have seen any 'popular' book (as opposed to a definitely religious book), which has even seen the possibility of a 'theological' faith as the true explanation of our life.

I wonder if you recognise, or are interested in recognising, how closely your book images the principles of the 'Athanasian Creed' – the twofold necessity of faith in the Trinity of God and the Incarnation.[1]

I wonder, getting this far, whether you would mind if I venture some criticism; – two of some importance, two of minor importance.[2]

1) Re. the Trinity – 'man' in his own image, a mirror of the Triune': That is St Augustine, but he gives the Trinity as: 'Being, Knowing, Willing'.[3] 1. Being, the reality of an existing mind; 2. The Thought, Word (Logos), or Idea formed in the mind; 3. The Activity, Power, Energy by which the Thought is carried out. You can put it more commonly of things: 1. the thing which is real; 2. the Essence of it, which we seek to know; 3. its activity, what it

does, by which we know it. E.g. Genesis, 1.i–iii: 'God', 'said' (a formed idea), 'it was so' (by a long process).[4]

But in your statements you have missed out the first and substituted the second – *viz.* the Idea. Then you had to divide the third into Energy (begotten?) and Power. Surely these are the same.

It should be: first, there is the living and Eternal God, in Himself infinite, beyond knowledge, unapproachable, but second, revealed in the Creative Idea, in time and in the lively soul.

That point about Reality is fundamental. Crowds of people and of writers, talk of 'God' at times with much feeling, but do we mean anything by it, or is it more than a vague 'sort of something'?

Mr Laurence Irving implicitly denies that it – or that you – mean anything.[5] 'The Archangels [...] represent the Will of God, Fate, Providence, Accident, or what you will'.[6] 'What you will' – as if it made no difference. Now to us, whether all these unfortunate occurrences have a meaning somewhere in the purpose (will) of God and are not merely part of a blind mechanism of chance, seems just as momentous as to whether murder or crime are acts of a will or the product of a determinist behaviourism.

I broke my arm once. I did not ask 'why?' knowing God was not likely to tell me – though I might guess a bit – but believing in a Will of God, I know there was a purpose, and I could laugh over it. If it was just fate or accident, I could only cuss at them stupidly. Your William broke his back and, at 77, I find my mind going feeble, but I am quite happy over it.

Of course, people do take opposite views. The strange thing is that Mr Irving should jumble up four words Will and Providence, Fate and Accident, as if there were no difference, and he does not even pair them rightly.

My views on the matter, as a parson and lecturer, are of no moment but he is writing a Preface to your book. And if I understand you at all, your very purpose – emphatically– is to show that the salvation of a soul came in recognising, accepting, submitting to an Eternal Will, which is not the same as acquiescence in fate.[7]

All would be unintelligible that way: I hope I have understood you rightly.

3) It seems a very small matter, but the byplay with the young cherub jars on me for various reasons.[8]

(a) Smart young things shocking their elders (or parsons) have been a stock joke in *Punch* for the last 40 years. Are the elders shocked or bored?

(b) 'Instructing youth' for nearly 50 years, the greatest difficulty seems to be in getting them to realise that there are reasons (or causes) worth asking for, thence, their passion for rhetorical questions, (like the serpent in Genesis 3. i. or Pilate); virtually assuming that there are no reasons. (Note, why do the angels assume that the cherub's question was a 'criticism' and not a genuine question?).

(c) Is it quite consistent that Michael, who 'never heard of such a thing', answers precisely the same question patiently and fully later on?[9]

4) I am not quite sure why you give this last answer to Michael. As I understand Scripture, the redemption of men by the Incarnation was a bit of a puzzle to the angels ('desire to look into'). According to a very attractive speculation the fall of Lucifer ('our lost brother') began as a refusal to accept that lost crowning with glory (of men).[10] Does the answer not belong rather to the Prior, who saw the point well enough but did not follow it up?[11] There is a technical difficulty. Sin is a whole and a Confessor cannot give Absolution in bits. In substance, you are right, the Prior's speeches here are rather wonderful.[12] Only the Voice of God himself could have broken through that resistance of the will.

In conclusion, please let me thank you for saying so much, and so well, what, as a dumb theologian and lecturer, one has struggled vainly to get across to people. I hope you will excuse if I have pressed my theological criticisms unduly.

[Herbert Kelly]

[1] The background to many of Kelly's comments here can be discerned in his series of lecture notes *De Trinitate* composed initially in 1911–12 and rewritten in 1932 (SSM/HK/LS/D/4/7 and 8).

[2] HK gives page references in the following paragraphs. These have been updated in the footnotes to correspond to the new publication: Dorothy L. Sayers, *The Zeal of Thy House* (Oregon, WIPF & Stock, 2011), pp.124 & 130.

[3] St Augustine, *De Trinitate*. Most commonly St Augustine's three powers of the soul are described as 'memory', 'understanding' and 'will'. One of the series of lectures Kelly prepared for Kelham students was on *De Revelatione* and *De Trinitate* (BI SSM/HK/LS).

[4] In the final scene of the play the archangel Michael explains the earthly trinity corresponding to the heavenly one as consisting of: Creative Idea, Creative Energy and Creative Power: Sayers, *Zeal*, p. 130–1. See also Genesis 1: i–iii: 'In the beginning God created the heavens and the earth […] God said […] and there was […].

[5] Laurence Irving (1897–1988), artist, set designer and director, who wrote the Preface to the first edition of *Zeal*, pp. 25–6.

[6] Sayers, *Zeal*, p. 26.

[7] Ibid. pp. 125-6.

[8] Ibid. pp. 73–4.

[9] It is all the angels who say in chorus: 'Criticising God's creation! I never heard of such a thing!' Ibid, p. 74 and pp. 120–24.

[10] Ibid. p. 74.

[11] Ibid. pp. 116–7.

[12] Ibid. p.114–8.

Letter 2   24 Newland Street
DLS to HK   Witham
                                                  Essex

4 October 1937

Dear Father Kelly,

Before I attempt, in the medieval manner, to 'defend my thesis', let me thank you most sincerely for your kind and sympathetic understanding of what I was trying to do in *Zeal of Thy House*. I have been pleased, touched, and also amused by many friendly reviews, announcing that the play was 'about' this, that or the other; but it is with a deep chuckle of delight that I greet the discovery, by an isolated person here and there, that this is actually a play 'about' that dusty and disagreeable thing, Christian Dogma. The neglect of dogma is the curse of nearly all Christian plays, from the playwright's point of view. The dogma of the Incarnation is the most dramatic thing about Christianity, and indeed the most dramatic thing that ever entered into the mind of man; but if you tell people so, they stare at you in bewilderment. Yet one would think (to adapt Voltaire) that if the Incarnation had never happened, it would have been necessary for some dramatist to invent it. However, since it is not the playwright's business to argue but to present, the only thing one can do is put it on the stage (in any form the Censor of Plays will permit) and let it speak for itself.

In this case, there was no doubt at all about the dramatic effect of the final scene in which Michael argues the matter out with William. It held the house attentive and excited, though there is absolutely no movement on the stage and the whole action is contained in the dogmatic argument. But it was interesting to discover, as I did, how many people (whether nominal Christians or not) either were Arians or believed that the Church taught a purely Arian doctrine.[1] However often they heard or recited the Creeds, it had obviously never sunk into their minds that Christ was supposed to be God in any real sense of the word. The Good and Suffering Man was a familiar idea to them: but the idea of a Suffering God was a staggering novelty. This isn't exaggeration – some of them quite simply and innocently told me so – especially some of my own actors, who, having seen the play through two months of rehearsal and ten performances, had had plenty of time in which to chew it over. I explained as much as I could (doing my best to steer clear of Sabellianism[2] and Patripassianism[3] and all the other terrifying heresies which lie in wait for amateurs who try to explain things over the lunch table), assuring them that the doctrine really was that Christ was always and equally God and Man. But I had to remind them that I was a playwright and not a theological expert and should certainly go wrong if I tried to express the matter otherwise than in my own craft, and beg them, if they really wanted to know, to go to somebody better qualified. I took the line that I wasn't asking them to believe anything (because earnest middle-aged females imploring young men to believe things do more harm than good) but that the play was meant to be a statement of what the doctrine really was, after which they could take it or leave it. It does seem just as well, if you are going to disbelieve a thing, to find out exactly what you are disbelieving. And I do honestly think we have heard a great deal too much recently about the 'Human Jesus'. That attractive and picturesque figure has almost succeeded in pushing the Divine Logos off the stage altogether, with the result that God the Father appears as the villain of the piece, which isn't orthodox. For my angel Cassiel – a young professional actor, who had been brought up a Unitarian – the play was a most peculiar experience! Being condemned, poor dear, to stand and listen for an hour-and-three-quarters trussed up in a pair of wings, while the characters argued about the nature of Christ, he could at first make neither head nor tail of what was going on. But, having a very sensitive and intelligent mind, he applied himself to working the thing out, and found it most surprising and interesting.

One thing that interested me was to discover a new application of that much disputed Athanasian statement that 'this is the Catholic faith, which except a man believe faithfully, he cannot be saved'. Artistically speaking, it turns out to be a plain statement of fact. I mean that unless you keep the God–Man idea properly balanced, your play, as a mere piece of dramatic structure, falls to pieces and makes no artistic sense: which brings me to the defence of my thesis; because the play is really chiefly 'about' the Christian dogma as it presents itself to the creative artist.

And therefore 1) The speech about the Trinity. This isn't meant to be a restatement of St Augustine (whose illustration, if I ever knew it, I had forgotten). It is, I'm afraid, only an effort of my own to make an illustration of three-in-oneness familiar to every creative artist and drawn from his own experience. (The play, by the way, was written to fit in with the Festival of Arts and Crafts at Canterbury, and that it why it is all about craftsmen). St Augustine says that God, in making Man, made an image of the Triune. I am trying to say that Man (made a Craftsman in the image of the Master-Craftsman) in making a work of art presents also an image of the Triune, because every work of creation is threefold.[4] Now it is a fact that when you set out to make a book (or anything else, of course, but I naturally tend to think in terms of books), you are simultaneously making three books, which are all the same book:

a) The Book as You Think it, which I have called the Idea (In the ordinary not the philosophical sense). This presents itself all at once, in a dispassionate kind of way, with the end and the beginning all there together, a timeless sort of thing with no distinguishable parts, just existing (here, I suppose, one links up with St Augustine) as if it had always been there and always would be.

b) The Book as You Write it. You can't have the idea without, at the same time seeing it as a sequence in time and a struggle with the material. This I have called the Energy, and it is, quite literally, 'begotten of that Idea' from the beginning, because the one without the other is unthinkable. The energy produces, of course, a visible 'incarnation' of the book in material form, but it exists before that and goes on after, so that it and the Idea co-exist inevitably and are still the same book.

c) The Book as You and They Read it. This is the most difficult to explain. I have called it the Power. It isn't the same thing as the Energy, though it proceeds (in the most orthodox manner) from the Idea and the Energy together. It is the thing that you give out to your readers* and your readers give back to you; and it, too, exists from the beginning, because every book is written for somebody, so that there is a partial exchange of Power going on.

> * [Sayers inserts a footnote to her letter here] Of course, to make the analogy go on all fours, the artist should have created his own public, but that is only true metaphorically. Still, all analogies break down somewhere, because if anything were exactly like another thing at all points it would be the thing. Even if St Athanasius' illustration about

the 'reasonable soul and flesh' lands you in awful difficulties about human reason if you take it literally.

I mean you can't write a book in *vacuo*: even if every other person in the world were annihilated, the writer would always be his own reader, so to speak. So that your own book comes back to you, as it were, from the minds to which it is addressed – still the same book, but with a different personality, 'neither confounding the persons nor dividing the substance'.

But Idea, Energy Power – it is always the same book; at least, it would be in an ideally perfect book, though as William truly observes, 'no man's work is perfect'[5], and often the Idea is feeble, the Energy ill-directed and the answer conspicuously lacking. But the writer would, I think, recognise the illustration as being sufficiently expressive of his own experience to serve as an illustration – no more, of course, than that. And if you were to ask him which of the three was 'the real book' – as Thought, as Written or as Read – he could only say 'each and all of them,' because you can't really separate them, even in thought.

Perhaps this explanation sounds even feebler than the original statement, but I did want to make it clear that I wasn't just jumbling up St Augustine but trying to work out a little picture of my own – very limited, naturally – of an earthly three-in-Oneness. There may be several illustrations for the same thing, mayn't there? – though I absolutely refuse to accept St Patrick's shamrock! Each leaflet of the shamrock *isn't* equally by itself the whole leaf, and you can't reasonably say that any one of them is begotten of, or proceeds from, another, because they all proceed alike from something quite different!

2. Mr Laurence Irving, bless his heart! Oh, dear – well, there you are! I've told him a hundred times that the play was about DOGMA, but, you see, he won't believe it. He thinks it's terrifically dramatic in spite of the dogma – and when people write prefaces to your book for you, you can't very well say 'Hi! that's not what it means to me.' He may reply, 'Well that's what it means to *me*.' (Apparently 'the Power' hasn't provoked quite the right

'response in the living soul' in his case!) His kindly intention was, I'm sure, to keep readers from being put off by the notion that the play might be about DOGMA. No doubt he feels that the world will accept God more easily if you call Him something else (like the editor in G.K.C's story, who crossed out the word 'God' wherever it occurred and substituted 'Circumstances').[6] I didn't expostulate with him (though I should enjoy it immensely if someone else did). For one thing my sense of humour got the better of me. For another, that book will go to theatrical managers, who will be much more inclined to give the play a London production if they don't think it's about that dreadful DOGMA. This consideration is highly immoral, but this is the point where, like William, one damns one's soul for the good of the work.

3. The Cherub and 4. Michael. These two points are part of the same thing. For dramatic purposes I've adopted the very idea you mention, viz: that, to the Angels, the whole business of Man's creation and Redemption is a puzzle. But they know it isn't their business to solve puzzles. I have tried to depict them as perfect but limited beings, each doing his own specialised job obediently without speculation or question. Raphael occupies himself with prayer; he can distinguish between true and false (William's devoted craftsmanship is recognised by him as having more of the true spirit of prayer than Theodatus's self-righteous litanies) – but his function does not extend further. Gabriel, the Heavenly messenger, intervenes in human affairs from time to time (as when he speaks in the ear of Ernulphus or as in the 'rope scene'), and he has a touch of that heavenly humour which makes the non-conformist mind so indignant. Cassiel records with austere im-partiality and can distinguish between the sin itself and the good use to which God may turn it. Michael's job is to deal out rewards and punishments and 'justify the ways of God to Man.' Therefore, when he is deputed to deal faithfully with William, he knows how to give him the appropriate theological instruction. But if William had gone further and asked, as the Young Cherub asks, 'Why did God create man at all, and with this particular nature?' Michael

could only say: 'I do not know. I am a soldier; I take my orders, and my orders are to deal with man as I find him. If you want to know anything outside revealed religion, you must not ask me. Possibly the College of Seraphim may know, but I do not, and I am not supposed to ask.'

Hence the rebuke to the Young Cherub: Angels must not ask that kind of question: that leads to the fall of Lucifer; man, indeed, asked questions, and that (for some inscrutable reason) led to the Incarnation, but Angels are angels and Men are men and it would never do for an angel to behave like a man. As a matter of fact, William never asks the Cherub's question; it would never occur to him, the artist, to ask Why another Artist chose to create anything, however fantastic or unusual. The love of making things for their own sakes is to him a perfectly sufficient and self-evident reason.

5. Your last point is about the Prior.[7] It has to be Michael, not the Prior, who finally copes with William's trouble, because Michael knows, as the Prior does not, what the trouble is. The Prior, you see, never heard William's outburst of ῦβϱΙς.[8] He does not, like the rest of them, commit himself to the easy assertion that the fall is a judgment for the Ursula affair. He knows God is usually a bit more subtle than that, so he puts the blame where, humanly speaking, it belongs and leaves it at that. But he feels a spiritual snag in William, only, as he says, he 'cannot read the heart' and isn't very sure where it is. And William is by this time incapable of telling him. (Ursula knew it at the time, of course; but her own sense of guilt over the accident has made her lose sight of it). William quite honestly doesn't see what the Prior is getting at. It is true there was an accident, due to somebody's perfectly plain carelessness, and in spite of it, here he is – crippled, certainly, but still able to work, obviously preserved because he is indispensable and carrying on very creditably under great difficulties – he really cannot see how anyone can find anything to blame him for (except, of course, those cheerful faults on which the Church is always so severe and which he is so sorry for). And since William really does seem to feel no conviction of sin, the Prior feels he

can't refuse him Absolution merely because he (the Prior) only thinks there is something else behind. He can only exhort him to self-examination, and when this fails, absolve him and hope for the best, adding at the same time the warning that Sacraments are not magic, acting independently of the will of the penitent. The Prior isn't really absolving him 'in bits', though I admit that the thought is rather condensed; he is only reminding him of the conditions under which any Sacrament is valid. (I don't think the Prior thinks William is making a bad confession; I think he recognises that he is only in a state of complete ignorance of himself). The confession scene is already rather long in performance, and there isn't room for a detailed discussion about Sacraments, and since there is a deeply rooted conviction in most people's minds that Sacraments are magic, working *ex opere operato,* possibly a slight over-emphasis in the other direction may do no great harm. But I might try to get this clearer, if it can be done in a line and a half! Of course, the minute Michael puts his finger on the seat of the trouble, William is up in arms. God has no right to take that attitude. And, after all, if it wasn't for the Incarnation, I don't know that He would have the right. But if God has really been through the whole grim business Himself, then He's fairly won the right, and one must give in – and that's why it's so exciting and dramatic, and why anybody should think that sort of doctrine DULL passes my comprehension. You may call it a fairy tale, but it's ridiculous to call it dull.

I didn't mean this letter to draw out into such a fearful screed. Such is the vanity of craftsmanship that any expression of interest or approval provokes them to shocking outburst of egotism. And I can't tell you how glad I am that you (on the whole) think well of the play and were kind enough to write and say so. It's always perilous for laymen to meddle with theology; but I gather you find the Incarnation part of it reasonably sound, and I hope you will allow the Trinity illustration, even though it's not St Augustine's, but only a sort of marginal note on my own copybook. I gave myself a fairly free hand over the Angels, because we don't seem to know much about them that's necessary to faith, so I gave them those attributes which seemed most useful dramatically.

The Archangels in Zeal of thy House, Canterbury Cathedral 1937

If the play is performed in London after Christmas, will you come and see it? Harcourt Williams (William)[9] and Anthony Quayle[10] (Michael) have promised to play in it again, and they are simply magnificent. I think you would like my angels – they stand eleven feet high in their wings and blaze with gold and colour. And with all its faults, the play does come off as a play. People come away from it with the idea that religion is interesting and exciting and practical, and not just a kind of dreary and sloppy emotion about something that has nothing to do with life. I'm sure it's full of theological slips, but it can't be worse for people than the perfectly incredible accounts of the Christian religion one gets in so many books and plays. The great thing is to get people interested, and then they can go on to ask their questions in the right quarter. They are all asking questions – especially the young men – and it's a funny thing, but practically any play that has so much as a whiff of any sort of religion about it can get an audience in London. Look at *Murder in The Cathedral* – look even at *The First Legion*, which is all about Jesuits and miracles and hasn't a woman character in it, and which everyone said would be off in a week, and it did quite well at Daly's (of all places) and is carrying on cheerfully at the Cambridge, which is a beastly theatre to play in.

Well, please forgive my inflicting all this upon you, and thank you very much.

Most gratefully yours,
Dorothy L. Sayers

[1] The belief, promulgated by the Alexandrian presbyter Arius (c. 256–336) which places emphasis on God's unity as opposed to Trinity – one being in three persons. God alone is self-existent, and the Son was created by him and from him. This doctrine was denounced as a heresy by the Council of Nicaea in 325, but the misunderstanding, as Sayers articulates it, has continued to permeate Christianity throughout the ages.

[2] The contested belief that Father, Son and Holy Spirit are three different forms or modes of God (also known as Modalism).

[3] The same belief in the Eastern Church.

[4] Sayers, *Zeal*, pp. 130–1. She develops this thought in her 1941 collection of essays: Dorothy L. Sayers, *The Mind of the Maker* (London: Continuum, 1994), pp. 26–35.

[5] Sayers, *Zeal*, p. 121.

[6] G. C. K. Chesterton, 'The Purple Wig', in *The Wisdom of Father Brown* (1914).

[7] Sayers, *Zeal*, pp. 113–30.

[8] Hubris, excessive pride or overconfidence.

[9] Harcourt Williams, 1880–1957, was DLS's personal choice for the role of William. He assisted in the shaping of the play from its inception and was also producer. Williams was to go on to produce and act in her second play for the Canterbury Festival, *The Devil to Pay,* in 1939.

[10] Antony Quayle, 1913–1989, English stage and film actor, he played the role of Michael very early in his career.

Letter 3   [House of the Sacred Mission
HK to DLS   Kelham Hall
                                                    Newark, Notts]

14 October 1937

Dear Miss Sayers

 I am always shy – was brung up that way – but this time I must
write. I enjoyed your book mighty, but nothing to the joy I got out
of your letter.
A. I have something I MUST say to yourself.
B. There are things I OUGHT to say on the 'doctrines' discussed.
C. And I should LIKE to say on little points.

A. First

 You say it is the business of a dramatist to present, but not
explain. That is absolutely right, but could you not do both?
Shakespeare stands out saying: NO – as many have noticed.
Bernard Shaw does both; saying something in a play, and telling
you what it is in a preface. You did – seemingly – at luncheon.[1]
Privately, I am going to get your letters copied, just to pass round
these boys – unless you object.

 Personally, I am literarily incompetent. I cannot read B.S., nor
his prefaces (except *Joan of Arc*). If you – as a literary person – lift
up your hands, and shout 'NEVER', I daresay you are right.
Things soak in, and if one tries to jam them in, folks just resent it.
Also – if there is a chance of getting this on the London stage,
perhaps it is better not to imperil it by frightening people. I leave
that to you entirely.

 What fills me with horror is the absolute truth of your remark
on how little 'Christian' people have grasped what their Creeds are
saying.[2] Me (HK) at Swanwick (1912): 'There is more Godlessness
to the square foot here than anywhere in England. You are all
talking of the 'Personality of Jesus', and it is merely admiration,
not faith – saint-worship, as of a magnified St Francis. I am talking
of GOD – and a Gospel – news. We are struggling to come to

God – and God has come to man; breaking our hearts over evil and God bore it'.[3]

A boy of ours in camp (1915) said: 'and they were all grousing at "religion", parsons, middle class'. I said I quite agree with you, but – he went off on his Creed – God the Creator; God, the Son of God, made man, died and rose; God the Power of God, working in us. Then a middle-aged corporal replied: 'That is too good to be true. I wish I could believe it, but I can't. Anyhow the parsons don't believe it, or they'd have told us.'

F.D. Maurice taught (I got it fifty-five years ago) 'we are all talking about religion, and men need to hear of God.'[4] I put it to old Bishop Talbot: 'The real trouble is that to them God is an ideal, a law, (fate or circumstance); He is not *real* enough to get In-carnate'.[5] Even to us parsons, it is more a matter of correct orthodoxy than a living conviction. You have no idea how difficult it is to get these boys (brought up in the strictest tradition of Anglo Catholic parishes) to see that it is a faith to be lived and used, not merely a formula to be stated, argued if necessary. That is where your letter is going to be a mighty help.

B.1

Now I am going on to our main doctrine points, and a lot of little ones concerning which you say a great deal about being an amateur not an expert – what strikes me is quite otherwise. I long to ask you: Where DID you get it all? I do not ask, because it is absurd to expect you to give me a soul's autobiography, but if I can persuade you to give your 'explanation' some time, a personal bit about how you came to see things this way – well, you can present the personal drama, and that is a mighty help.

Yes – the letter is amateur. There are all sorts of little 'breaks' I want to put in. You may know all about them, but – if I shove them in – they may interest you.[6] Small points: Voltaire – Incarn-ation – 'some dramatist to invent it.'[7] That is just what they did do. All the heathen myths were attempts that way: 'Let us suppose – once upon a time – Ares, etc. came down and fought, among men'

(Homer etc.). The one thing you cannot invent is: 'it happened – in the fifteenth year of Tiberius etc.'.

You refer to: – 'how many are Arians'. Arius did not teach the modern humanist Christ, but a 'Divine being'; Wells' 'invisible king': not God at all – Divine, but not deity.[8] Worthy of *hyper-dulia* (the R.C. term for worship due to the Blessed Virgin Mary – something above saints, but short of God). I am never sure how far these people who talk of a 'unique personality' etc. really mean mere man. That is the effect of it. The real motive is the dread men have of coming too near. A young ordinand got talking with one of my boys and said: 'The worst of your view is that it would bring God into everything'. Terrible that. People want God – but up in heaven, out of the way. I call it the 'externality of God'.[9]

B.2 *De Trinitate*

Yes. God in everything. *Ibi est trinitas.* 'All human life is dualism, and all reality is a Trinity'.[10] Dualism – conflict or opposition of the irreconcilable – facts and theories – rule and freedom, etc. I wonder if, as a writer, you have noted the literary sanctity of 'threes'. Baroness Orczy wrote: 'Rain, rain, rain: monotonous, weary, depressing.'[11] Rain – three times. If she had used four times, the effect is different. Then you should say: 'A and B, C and D.' Laurence Irving gives four, but does not pair them'.[12] The Baroness' adjectives are 'in procession' – monotonous, in fact; suggesting weariness of the mind; depression in the feelings.

I am sorry, but I found your exposition difficult at first, then I tumbled to it completely: 1. Thought 2. Writing 3. Reading. It just fell in with an idea I was noting (re. Vocation) on the Will, which is 1. Desire 2. Conceiving a Purpose 3. Proceeding in Action. Analogy of human and divine.[13] 1. Our 'Thoughts' (and Desires) are a muddle of inconsistencies: in God each is one whole. 2. Few of ours ever come to expression (or purpose); in God the expression is co-equal, and 3. The work is in God, perfect, even if, in time, it is very long.

Do you know Aquinas' distinction of 'conceived' and 'proceeding'? 'There are two forms of procession: The Father 'conceives' the Son, a single whole image of himself, Logos or purpose, (expression), but the spirit works in 'manifold forms'. There is no *single* embodiment, (Incarnation); 'procession' is the only word you can use. (I quite agree re. the shamrock. I suppose you know the pre-Augustinian parallels: sun, ray, light; OR Fountain, stream. water).[14]

I wonder if you know Fr Benson (of Cowley): 'The decay of Christendom began when the Middle Ages shut up the Doctrine of the Trinity in Latin treatises for the clergy'.[15] Hence, secondary matters, and 'the circulating life of the Godhead was no longer thought of. It has meant a great deal to me.

Irving. Yep. Quite so. Mos' amusin'. Looks to me like one of those people who think 'drama' is a way of putting things, not a quality of the things themselves. Is that not common among journalists? It is among preachers.

Also, yes. I see your point [on obedience] and yet I don't. I do not believe in the approach: soldiers obey orders – 'theirs not to reason why' (Boer War, etc.). It has cost the army an awful lot. The professional's devotion to the approved way of doing things is the reason why the amateurs give the professionals such a bad time. That is the danger of all professionalism, including parsons. In SSM it is laid down: 'It is not enough to do what you are told; you must seek what you are told, understand it, why it is wanted. Then you will know how to deal with it'.[16] See book of Job. He was bent on asking 'why'. Only two things are needed: While you must understand what you have to do; you must not be upset if you don't get it. You write that it is 'perilous for laymen to meddle with theology'. It is a bit too 'parson' – as if the vital thing were to get it correct, rather than to understand its life. If you do not risk your knuckles knocking, the door will not open.

Regarding Confession: I talked it over with *our* Prior[17], who knows far more of it than I do. The only technical criteria is that you can only give absolution positively; he could not give it generally 'for the sins you have confessed.' But he also agreed with me – in agreeing with you – that you are absolutely right on the main point. If the Confessor did know what was wrong, he may not push it, if the penitent does not. Outside of confessions he can say (Buchman would): 'What's wrong with you is not that, but.... etc'.[18] It is the very real difficulty of confession, that you can only confess acts. Here again, the 'correct' definition – 'sin is an act against the commandments of God' – is utterly wrong. As you make plain – the acts were foolish. The real sin was a state of mind.[19]

I can hardly imagine that you have read any books of mine. There are only two going, and neither have attracted any notice (except from the Archbishop of York). One is called the *Gospel of God*, in which I tried to expound just your 'theology'. The other, called *Catholicity*, has a final chapter on Confession, where I pressed just your point.[20] N.B. This is another of those matters where, I think, folk want your explanation badly.

I want to add another crit. on those pages. There is a bit too much on the Crucifixion.[21] (Not a crit. really, I misdoubt if you could have said more, it is rather an addendum for your thinking). S. Anselm set the medieval mind on the crucifixion as the great 'satisfaction' or 'paying off' for sin. Cranmer etc. accepted it. The Evangelicals made it central. But it was not patristic nor Pauline. Note that it is built on the externality of God – as someone Who makes rules, conditions, etc. for us to keep and Who judges. The Cross 'atones' for sin, in the ordinary sense, where unity, at-one-ment has been forgotten. In Cranmer's Prayer Book (1552–1662),[22] only the sacrifice is alluded to, but if you have a 1928 version handy, look at the 'Wherefore having in remembrance – Incarnation, Passion, Resurrection, Ascension, Session, etc.' It is one whole thing by which man and God are made at one. The simplest is the *Te Deum*: 'When Thou didst deliver man, – the Virgin's womb: when Thou hadst overcome the sharpness of death, Thou didst open etc.' Not Friday, but Sunday, is the outstanding Christian day.

'Now, finally my dear brethren', please don't imagine my crits. imply only a modified approval. There is only one sentence I stick at: 'peril to a layman meddling with theology.' Laymen *ought* to. I would to God that one-tenth of the experts had anything like your grip on the essentials of the question. I have stuck in a lot of my favourite 'tweaks', because I thought you would like them, and (here and there) they might help you. If you knew them all before (I half expect you may), it does not really take long to run through.

[Herbert Kelly]

---

[1] This comment refers to her remark in the previous letter about 'amateurs who try to explain things over the lunch table'.

[2] In *History of a Religious Idea*, a pamphlet written by HK in 1898, he writes: 'In an age of uncertain acquiescence, at once Pantheistic and Unitus, to disparage logic is suicidal […]. We have been careful to adhere strictly and loyally to the authoritative teaching of the Church of England, believing that to be in truth Catholic, Scriptural, and reasonable' and 'The Creed is in three parts – (a) What is God? What is an Infinite Will? There cannot be a world-order except around that Will. But how can man come to it? It is plain he cannot, but (b) there is a Gospel telling us that God came to man, and took his World-Order to Himself, redeemed it – not, as we always think, by "what He does," but by what He suffered – and out of that made Triumph and Ascension. (c) But in as much as we are separate beings with independent wills, choices, judgements, what we have we, or can we have, in a common Redemption? How is this Infinite Will, Eternal and Universal, related to the individual will?' He also opined that the creeds 'have nothing to do with opinions, but a belief *in*. They attempted only to make clear what was the meaning of that "thing" in which we trusted, what we trusted it for', quoted in Dewey, 'SSM Chronicle', p. 93.

[3] From 1908 HK took students every year to the Student Christian Movement (SCM) at Swanwick. He wrote up notes of the conferences and his own responses to the meetings. The 1912 event he described as: 'the dullest camp I have ever been at to my recollection' but it brought home to him, 'the immense importance of this movement'. Although the quotation that he cites here cannot be found it was likely concerning the discussions around the person of Jesus. He commented: 'We were enormously occupied over our own [experience] but I never heard anyone in Camp talk about God, except incidentally, though [there was] any amount about Jesus Christ. We all started from the Person of Jesus Christ, beauty, magnificence etc. etc. Then we went on to ask, 'who was this person?' […]. All their talk of the Person of Jesus Christ and of magnificences, and beauties, – I can see it was pious and I suppose it was elevating, but it bored me to distraction. I was sick of the very name of St Francis. You talk to me about God and I listen. Talk to me about your extra superfine saints, make Jesus Christ the ideal man and I am not even interested. I'm mightily interested in small men, common men, real men; I've always understood that it was for them in especial [sic] that Christ died'. (SSM-

HK-SCM/4 and 5, pp. 233–6. See also George Every, 'Father Kelly and the S.C.M. 1907-1950' in *The Student Movement,* January-February 1951, pp. 26–7 (SSM/HK/BIO/BP/6/8).

[4] Fredrick Denison Maurice (1805–1872), Anglican theologian. HK wrote of Maurice's influence on his thinking especially relating to the Creeds: 'Maurice's phrase was "I am not so much interested in men's systems (doctrines or conclusions) as in their method." So it was with Maurice himself. It was not his doctrines - I never saw that he had any special to himself - it was the way he reached them, and the use he made of them... The subsoil determines the character of the soil, and if you want to build on the rock, you must dig, and not be content with surface trenches. I was seeking the infinite truth of the creeds, as that which underlay life', quoted in Dewey, 'SSM Chronicle', p. 14. (Also see SSM/HK/BIO/AB).

[5] Edward Talbot (1844–1934), in turn bishop of Rochester, Southwark and Winchester. Some correspondence with Talbot is in the SSM archives, (SSM/HK/SP/25/1).

[6] HK's style is very difficult to follow here. This letter has been edited to try and convey his arguments without the numbers and repetitions which confuse and distract.

[7] He is referring to the opening paragraph of DLS's letter.

[8] H.G. Wells, *God the Invisible King,* 1917.

[9] The centrality of God, not religion, was a perpetual theme of HK's writing, see Introduction.

[10] Herbert Kelly, *De Trinitate,* introductory notes, II, bound lecture scheme (SM/HK/LS/8/2).

[11] Baroness Emmuska Orczy, *The Scarlet Pimpernel,* chapter xliii (1905).

[12] In his introduction to *Zeal,* 'Will of God, Fate, Providence, Accident', p. 26.

[13] A typescript in the archives by HK, dated 7th October 1937, deals with 'the will of God and man' and discuss the will in Trinitarian terms. This issue was clearly central to his thinking at the time. 1937 'S.S.M. Vocation' typescript, 3pp (SSM/HK/SSM/71).

[14] Thomas Aquinas, *Summa Theologica,* Question 36, The Person of the Holy Spirit.

[15] This is a favourite quotation of Kelly's. He cites it in his description of the Kelham Course (published in SSMQ Michaelmas 1937 and Easter 1938, SSM/QP/9). The original statement by Richard Meux Benson cannot be identified.

[16] It is not clear where this statement comes from. There are similar instructions in the *Principles* of SSM and in the *Constitutions.*

[17] Stephen Bedale. He was appointed Prior in 1923.

[18] HK is referring here to Frank Buchman (1878–1961) the American born Lutheran pastor who was the inspiration for the founding of the Oxford Group in the 1920s and later for the Moral Re-Armament Movement. Kelly wrote a series of articles on the Oxford Group (see Letter 28, note 2).

[19] HK is not expressing his point well here, perhaps he meant to say: What is confessed in the 'act' includes the understanding of the gravity of the act as well as the intention in committing it.

[20] Herbert Kelly, *The Gospel of God* [first published 1928] (London: SCM, 1959) and *Catholicity* (London, SCM, 1932), pp. 147–158.

[21] Presumably HK is referring to the last speeches of Michael and William.
[22] The Book of Common Prayer.

Letter 4   24 Newland Street,
HK to DLS   Witham,
                                                    Essex.

20 October 1937

Dear Father Kelly,

Thank you very much indeed for your long and friendly and most stimulating letter. I was really ashamed when I thought what a fearful great screed I had sent you to wrestle with.

One thing I expressed badly. I am all for encouraging laymen to meddle with theology on their own account – the more they go in for a little hard thinking as a change from woolly emotionalism the better. I should have said, 'it is perilous for laymen to meddle with *expounding* theology' – it is so easy to get confused and give a totally wrong impression, owing to lack of practice in handling technical terms.

That is one of the reasons why I feel sure that the artist's business is to present and not to expound (I'd back Shakespeare against Shaw every time!). Another is, that when the dramatist abandons his own technique and starts to argue, he is apt to lose grip on the thing, and become so eager to split hairs and justify himself that he fetters his own work. And thirdly, I believe people are more ready to be persuaded by a religious drama if it is not preceded by anything that looks like preachment.

Actually, in practice, I don't think any of the people who saw *Zeal of Thy House* acted were in much doubt about what I was trying to say as regards the Incarnation doctrine. What they found great difficulty in believing was that the doctrine, as presented, was orthodox C. of E. Their attitude was, not so much 'this is too good to be true' as 'this is too exciting to be orthodox'. Even if the book were prefaced by a certificate of orthodoxy signed by the entire bench of Bishops, they would probably not be persuaded.

Arians: Yes – I *think* Arians is about right – or let us say that the *highest* point most of them get to is to imagine that the Church's position is Arian. They range from a wholly 'human Jesus' up to a position in which they allow that 'some unique kind of divineness' is to be imputed to Jesus. What *exactly* they mean by this latter I don't know. One woman said: 'Isn't it the sort of divine spark that there is in all of us, only in a unique degree – the same thing only more so?' I said I thought that wasn't quite what was meant, because Christ was held to be the same – here the word 'person' loomed up like a trap, but I avoided it, since she *might* remember the Athanasian Creed and convict me of heresy – 'the same *personality* as God the Creator – the same *Thing*' – this sounded merely irrelevant – 'in fact the same God and just as much God – *really* God, in a very different way from you and me.' Which is where explanations land you. As a dramatist, of course, one just puts the idea over, not by explanation at all, but by re-iterated statement: 'Crucify God'; 'those […] Hands that bear the sharp nails' imprint and upheld the axis of the Spheres'; 'God bore this too'; God died' and so on – leaving them to draw the conclusion, 'if it was God who was crucified, then Christ = God.' But it isn't really the dramatist's job to say 'this is orthodox'; that's the parson's job.

I'm afraid I haven't read your books, but I will, especially as 'my' theology turns out (and I am very happy to know it) to be 'your' theology also. I didn't think it was 'my' theology exactly; I thought it was the Church's, so far as it went, and I am a little startled to hear that your 'brothers' find such a personal flavour about it. Bits of my expression of it (notably the Prior's speech about John and Peter) are indebted to G.K. Chesterton; but I think the body of it emerges quite simply from the Creeds – always provided that one starts by supposing that the Creeds were intended to mean something sensible and are not just a lovely rumbling of hypnotic sound, suitable for stupefying congregations: 'the Father incomprehensible, the Son incomprehensible and the Whole Thing incomprehensible', as the old tale has it.

De Trinitate: I admit that my use of the word 'Idea' is a little confusing – but only, I think, to theologians, not to the ordinary person, for whom it has no specialised metaphysical connotation. The artist uses it as I use it – you will notice that William is made to use it twice: 'I've had an idea about this' – thus 'planting' it (as we say) for later use in the Trinity speech.[1] The word you use, 'expression', would do admirably for the Second Person, but that, of late years, it has become horribly contaminated by 'expressionism' and 'self-expression', used to convey the pouring out of one's feelings higgledy-piggledy, without regard either to form or 'good form' – a meaning as far removed as possible from the blood and sweat and discipline of the genuine craftsman's 'energy'.

Prior: I'm glad that, on the main point, *your* Prior feels I've got hold of the right end of the stick. (The actor, by putting the right emphasis here, can help a lot to give the right sense). Most Protestants labour under the delusion that: 'It must be nice to be a Catholic, because you can get all your sins cleaned off by the priest every Saturday and start again'. (Or alternatively, of course, it must be dreadful because the priest has a high old time licking his lips over your sins in the Confessional and then pursuing them into your private life and brandishing them in your face so as to 'get a hold over' you).

Crucifixion: In a *play* (which only takes about two hours and has a story to tell) one can't give a complete exposition of Christian doctrine. One has to take the bit that is important *for the story* and concentrate on getting that 'planted' all through, so as to make its effect when the time comes. For *William*, the point where he comes smack up against it is that line 'For lo! God died, and still His work goes on'. Everything else has to be subordinated to that dramatic effect. But you'll notice I've left out all those disgusting ideas about 'satisfaction' and 'paying-off'. I've tied it up with the 'knowledge' question all through. Man says, 'You say I mustn't know – but I intend to know'. God replies, 'Very well. If you insist, I shall not prevent you; nor shall I annihilate My creation or stop My work on that account. But I have to inform you that the price of that particular kind of knowledge is toil, suffering, renunciation and death. And since I made you with free will (and what we make we love) I will stand by you. I will go every step of the way with you. Further, I will turn your evil to good, so that, in the end, and by holding on to Me, you will attain all, and more than all, I originally intended for you, and a 'crown such as the angels know not'.

Angels: that is why, dramatically, the Angels are made to stand so far apart from this business of 'wanting to know'. I quite agree that it is a pity for man to obey man implicitly; but for an Angel to take God's orders for granted isn't quite the same as for Tommy Atkins to take Colonel Blimp's orders for granted. (My professional actors, trained to display human passion, had a shattering task! 'You've got to imagine' (said I) 'that you are beings who have never known passion, grief, remorse, rebellion, irritability, doubt, hesitation, pain, sickness, fatigue, poverty, anxiety or any of the ills flesh is heir to: you may show a divine anger, but you mustn't sound cross; you may be tender, but on no account emotional; you may be joyful but not excitable; and although you have to stand for two mortal hours on a very hot day in heavy robes and uncomfortable wings, you must try hard to imagine that you have no bodies to speak of, that your legs do not ache, that your harness is not digging into your shoulders, that the sweat if not rolling down your faces and that two of you are not, in fact, sodden and streaming with hay-fever!' And very nobly they did it, poor lambs!).

Well, I *do* hope the play will come to Town, and that you may yet be able to see it – it *looks* so beautiful. I will see that you have the centre of the front row of the stalls, if you do come, and perhaps, with the electric contraption, you might hear some of it. My Michael has the grandest voice, like a silver trumpet – when he says 'all the Sons of God shouting for joy' it sounds like it! It is

good of you to say you will send people and will try and get TOC
H interested – that would be a tremendous help.[2] Of course, it's a
great job trying to get managers to do anything about a 'religious'
play – the very word fills them with dreary discomfort and sends
their financial spirits down to the soles of their boots. They don't
like Christ very much (since half of them are Jews, that is not so
very surprising).[3] They only know two versions of Him. There is
'gentle-Jesus-meek-and-mild' (dull, and suitable for Christmas
plays for amateurs) and there is 'Suppose-Christ-came-again-
today' (usually strongly Communistic and all about working-class
prophets in drab surroundings). But a Christianity with colour and
humour and suitable for use under ordinary conditions of life is a
very queer thing, for which they feel nobody is likely to pay good
money. As Lord Melbourne is once said to have remarked,
'Nobody has a greater respect for the Christian religion than I
have, but really, when it comes to intruding it into a gentleman's
private life…!'

Again, a thousand thanks for your great kindness and interest.
I am truly and deeply grateful.

Yours very sincerely,

[DLS]

P.S. 'Gentle-Jesus-meek-and-mild' has probably made more
apostates than any other single phrase in the language. And what
a phrase! About as adequate as calling a man-eating tiger 'poor
pussy'!

---

[1] William uses the word 'idea' once in Act 1 (p. 43) and later in Act 2 (p. 59). In
total, the word is used seven times before it is taken up by Michael in his
'Trinity' speech.
[2] TOC H (short for Talbot House) was an international Christian movement
founded in 1915. The founder was Philip Thomas 'Tubby' Clayton (1885–
1972). See Letters 16, 18, 19 and 21 below. There is no mention of TOC H in
HK's previous letter (nor of his deafness) which suggests an intervening
communication which has not survived.

[3] DLS has been accused of anti-Semitism by some commentators. Certainly, some of the portrayals of Jewish characters in her novels would be considered unacceptable today. It has been argued, not altogether convincingly, that she was reflecting the cultural attitudes of her time and that these did not necessarily represent her own views. See: Amy E. Schwartz, 'The Curious Case of Dorothy L. Sayers and the Jew Who Wasn't There', *Moment Magazine*, July/August 2016 and 'Dorothy L. Sayers', *New World Encyclopaedia*, https://www.newworldencyclopedia.org (accessed July 21, 2022).

Letter 5   Society of the Sacred Mission
HK to DLS   Kelham Theological College
                                                   Kelham
                                           Newark, Notts

23 Nov. 1937

My dear Miss Sayers

I did not write to thank you for the very intriguing post card photograph of your angels. Allow me to do so.[1] Once more, I am being pushed. I am going up on Friday for a week to my sister in London – Lady Long – and she asks me if I would like to ask you to tea in her flat.[2] Well, I should – if you are in London, and care to come down so far – any day Saturday to Tuesday inclusive.

I do not know if you are likely to be in London and have an afternoon free. Also, it is a bit out of the way: 57 Hurlingham Court, SW 6, about 100 yards from Putney Bridge Station. Go out of the station to the left – under the viaduct, and it is the first big barrack of flats on the right. If you are not likely to be up, I expect to be in London in Christmas week – if that suits you better.

Any prospects of the play coming out in London?

Yours sincerely in Christ,

[H Kelly]

A p.c. to Hurlingham Court would be safest.

[1] This has not survived.

[2] Maud Long, née Kelly, was HK's younger sister. She married Arthur Long in 1893. Brigadier general Sir Arthur Long (1866–1941) received the KBE, CB and CMG for service during the First World War. In the 1930s, HK advised on marital difficulties in her family (SSM/HK/C/F/10/15–18).

Letter 6   [24 Newland Street
DLS to HK   Witham
                                                      Essex]
25 November 1937

Dear Father Kelly,

I shall be in Town this weekend and shall, of course, be delighted to come and see you: it is most kind of Lady Long to invite me. May I come on Sunday afternoon, as that is the most convenient day for me? If I do not hear to the contrary, may I turn up at Hurlingham Court about four o'clock on Sunday? I may, by that time, have a little news about the London prospects of *The Zeal of Thy House*.

In case this time should not be convenient, my London address and telephone number are: 24, Great James Street, Bloomsbury, W.C.1. Holborn 9156.

Greatly looking forward to meeting you.

      Yours very sincerely
        [DLS]

Letter 7   Society of the Sacred Mission
Richard Roseveare SSM   (S. Bernard's Mission Church)
to DLS   42, Northlands Road
                                                Southey Green
                                                     Sheffield

8 February 1938

Dear Miss Sayers,

Let me introduce myself as the person who (quite accidently) was responsible for getting Fr Kelly to read *The Zeal of Thy House* and then write to you about it. He always contended that you would not answer his letter, but I felt I knew better and have been allowed to see the proof of my prophecy!

Last October I was sent here to take charge of a new venture of our Society at the invitation of the Bishop of Sheffield.[1] We are here (three of us) at the beginning of the foundation of a parish which is to have three churches and a population of about 50,000 people. As yet, only a small proportion of them are here – for once the dear old Church has got in first.

All I want of you, if I may ask you, is your permission to reprint a few of the pearls you have dropped in your article in the Ely Diocesan Appeal which has just reached me. The architect of the church at Cambridge is to build one of our three churches and he sent me the brochure.

I have taken the liberty of enclosing a copy of our parish magazine so that you will see the sort of thing I should be using in which to quote your words. We are rather proud of the production – not for its literary worth (for I have to write it all myself!) so much as for the layout which is an attempt to get away from the dreariness of the conventional mag.

If you have a moment, I should be so grateful if you could sign and seal your kind permission in the enclosed stamped and addressed envelope. You must be quite used to enclosing such things yourself for the return of MS from editors – in the very dim and distant past I suspect!

> Yours sincerely
>> Richard Roseveare SSM[2]
>> Priest in charge

---

[1] This was at Parson's Cross, a large housing estate in Sheffield. By 1941 there were seven brethren in the priory. The parish was given up in 1956. (SSM/PY/SPC/D).
[2] Richard Roseveare, 1902–1972, prior at Sheffield Priory and later Provincial in South Africa and Bishop of Accra.

Letter 8   [24 Newland Street
DLS to HK   Witham
                                                      Essex]

7 February 1938

Dear Father Kelly,

I know you will be glad to hear that *The Zeal of Thy House* is coming to London at the end of March: it is being put on by Mr Anmer Hall[1] at the Westminster theatre for a run of one month with Mr Harcourt Williams as William of Sens, and Mr Antony Quayle as Michael and one or two others of my original Canterbury cast. I do hope you will be able to come and see it and send as many friends as you can persuade. It is a little unfortunate that we have to begin in Lent and so close to Holy Week, since the first two weeks of a very short run are so important; we hope, however, that in view of its being a religious play, some good Christian people may be able to reconcile their consciences to going in Lent, and we shall, in any case, run on over Easter week, which ought to be a good one. Perhaps, later on, I may send you one or two posters and leaflets to display at Kelham. It is all very exciting, and I hope I shall do well with the show.

I continue to make interesting discoveries about Christian doctrine as understood by the laity; a young man of my acquaintance, brought up in some kind of Christianity, was astonished to hear that the Church considered pride to be a sin at all, having always been under the impression that sins of the flesh were the only sins that counted. He seemed to think that the main outline of the faith, as I endeavoured to explain them over a glass of sherry in a pub (I always seem to be expounding the faith in pubs!) was something quite revolutionary and unheard of, though interesting.

I had a very kind letter from Mr. Eric Fenn,[2] asking permission to give an amateur performance of the play at a Student Conference; in view of the London production, I had to refuse this permission, but he has very kindly undertaken to do all he can to help in getting publicity for our production.

With kindest remembrance,

Yours sincerely

[DLS]

---

[1] Alderson Burrell Horne (1863–1953), theatre director, who worked under the name Anmer Hall.

[2] Revd Eric Fenn, a Presbyterian minister, was Assistant Secretary to the Student Christian Movement (SCM) 1926–37. This letter does not appear to have survived but he had considerable correspondence with DLS later after his appointment as Assistant Director of Religious Broadcasting at the BBC in 1937. See Reynolds, *Letters, Vol II*.

Letter 9   House of the Sacred Mission,
HK to DLS   Kelham,
                                            Newark, Notts.

[February 1938]

My dear Miss Sayers,

Joy! I had begun to despair. I will do what I can, though your being pushed into the tail end of Lent for so essentially Catholic a play is indeed an irony. But I suppose you had to take it – it is a *religious* play as you say, but whether High Church folk will see it that way I don't know. I will do what I can.

1) My best 'vicar' (Fulham) is in hospital, alas. Exit.[1]

2) I put on Eric Fenn. I did not think you could rise to a private performance but hoped that amateurs nibbling [would] attract the professional fish. Anyway S.C.M. is a biggish organisation.

3) I am on with another request of very uncertain value – Mrs Maurice Bear (a cousin of mine) – been running various associations for many years – under the name of 'Wayfarers' – friends for the lonely.[2] These are mixed clubs which tend to concentrate on servants – Guilds for Mistresses, Servants, and Registries. It all looks very good to me, but somehow it doesn't seem to go. She is 74 and can't get anyone to take over. Rather sad. Perhaps too much Mrs M. B aforesaid! I wish I could find someone who knew of it and could tell me. She's a well-meanin' person, and (like William) I think, taking it a bit hard that her work is dropping away from her. It is sad.

Anyhow the point for you is that she edits a monthly *Wayfarers' Gazette*. If you could let me have a hand-bill – quick – I might get a notice in the March issue.

I wonder if you'd like to see my aforesaid Cousin. I'll send you papers if you'd like.

Yours sincerely in Christ
Herbert Kelly S.S.M

¹ Unknown.

² Mrs Maurice Bear (addressed as 'Georgie' in letter 14) and HK were related through their grandmothers who were sisters. Mrs Maurice Bear left a memoir of HK (SSM/HK/BIO/BP/21).

Letter 10   [24 Newland Street
DLS to HK   Witham
                                                      Essex]

17 February 1938

Dear Father Kelly,

Thank you so much for your letter. It is ironical, as you say about Lent; but it was that or nothing. I have at any rate succeeded in persuading the management that they cannot open in Holy Week. For the first ten days we shall have to enlist the help of my personal friends (mostly pagans) and of the non-conformists who, for some reason obscure to me, keep Holy Week as a kind of festival, culminating as a tea-fight on Good Friday: possibly there is some dim ritual connection with Hot Cross Buns!

I will certainly let you have a preliminary notice as soon as they are printed; the trouble is that the theatre is still struggling with the precise date, though I do not think myself there is much doubt that it will open on the 29ᵗʰ March. The special notices of the play will be printed a little later on, and I will then send you, if I may, a number to distribute; they will be quite small in size.

With many thanks
       Yours sincerely
              [Dorothy L. Sayers]

Letter 11   [24 Newland Street
DLS to HK   Witham
                                                          Essex]

21 February 1938

Dear Father Kelly,

The enclosed notices are all that is available at the present moment. It is, however, pretty safe to say that the first performance will be on March 29th. If Mrs Maurice Bear could see her way to putting a notice in the *Wayfarer's Gazette*, she may find it of interest to add that the leading parts of William of Sens and the Archangel Michael, will be played by Mr. Harcourt Williams and Mr. Anthony Quayle, as in the original Canterbury production. As soon as the actual leaflets devoted to *The Zeal of Thy House* are ready, I will send them along, but I fear that they will not be out in time for advance notice in magazines. They will, however, really contain no more than I have let you know already.

With many thanks,
            Yours very sincerely in Christ
                [Dorothy L. Sayers]

Letter 12   House of the Sacred Mission
HK to DLS   Kelham,
                                                Newark, Notts.

14 March 1938

Dear Miss Sayers

I cannot remember where we have got to, I think I did answer your letter of 7 Feb. I know I wrote to you of Mrs Maurice Bear —

of 'The Wayfarer's' because she has heard from you and has put a notice of the play in her *Wayfarers Gazette*, of which I assume you have been sent a copy.

I asked her if she would like to see you, and she replied by asking if I can get you to speak which takes me a bit faster than I was going. Stage ii should have been to ask *you* if you cared. However, here it is![1] I forget how much I told you. Mrs Bear is my cousin. [Her] family *were* Congregationals [sic] of Colchester. Maurice Bear (male) was in business in Calcutta (no children). Mrs B is a person of boundless energy – used to run all over India doing Girl Guides, and I don't know what else. Now they are retired, they used to live in Bombay; now I think both of them are running Clubs etc. for the lonely. Also Guilds in a triplet: (a) for servants; (b) for mistresses and (c) for agencies.

Now she is getting old (74 – tho' she don't look it) and – like your William – her work, which is her life, seems likely just to flop – come next May. She takes it a bit hard; for no one is ready to take it on. It will be as God wills – that was all I could say. All the same, it does not seem to me right and the human duty is to keep it going.

Her letter is a bit jittery. She has a dislike of committees – which she expects me to share. Well, I don't. I have heard too many people talk that way as an excuse for doing it all themselves. She knows of that and is anxious to show that she does *not* 'rule'. Oh, may be! Maybe its influence. I was conscious always that only an organisation or system could be permanent. There it is. I cannot do anything: too stupid; too ignorant. If you can/care to speak for her, it will be a help and cheer her.

If, knowing London and '*things*' – as I don't – you could get her to talk – if you can get a hint of what is wrong – give a hint of how it could get straight, well that's better still. I guess I have done the most I can. I hope to be in and about London from Easter for a week or two. Starting from my sister's Nursing Community at Highgate (the 'Sisters of Christ the Consoler').[2] Mother Jessie –

the superior – who belongs in Truro is a wonderful old lady.[3] If you are still thirsting for introductions she is worth knowing.

Yours sincerely in Christ

Herbert Kelly S.S.M

My pet study is 'predestination'; the relation of God's will to ours. Obviously: we must try to do God's will. But that is not a bit obvious: 1) we do not know God's will. He takes jolly good care we shouldn't. 2) It's not at all obvious for us to do. Does God mean that 'Wayfarers' should snuff out? Looks like it. BUT – its plain duty to keep on if we/she possibly can.

If you can't follow this up, let me have the letter back, but if you can and care to, you can stick to it as long as you want. Time enough to write if you can get anywhere/somewhere. Sorry to bother you with my troubles.

---

[1] The enclosed letter/invitation has not survived.

[2] The Nursing Community of Christ the Consoler (later known as the Community of the Presentation) was founded in 1927. The sisters combined nursing duties with praying the Divine Office in community. The Mother House at Highgate provided medical and convalescent facilities. See Peter Anson, *The Call of the Cloister* (London: SPCK, 1955), pp. 518–9.

[3] Mother Jessie had been a member of the Community of the Epiphany, founded in 1883, which HK's sister, Edith Mary, entered c.1919. M. Jessie became the first superior of the Nursing Community.

Letter 13
HK to Georgie
(Mrs Bear)

House of the Sacred Mission,
Kelham,
Newark, Notts.

25 March 1938

My dear Georgie

I wrote to Miss Sayers and got a gracious answer this morning. N.B. she writes awful nice letters – as if one was a life-long friend. I think she'll do what you ask, but ask her over – try to get her interested in the general bag of tricks. I would if I were you. Maybe she might help by giving a talk. She must know a power of people: She may know the one you're lookin' for.

Her London address (seemingly) is 24 Great James Street, W.C.1. Can't be far off you.

Your affectionate cousin
Herbert Kelly S.S.M

Letter 14
HK to DLS

House of the Sacred Mission
Kelham,
Newark, Notts

25 March 1938

Dear Miss Sayers

Have written to Mrs Bear. Regarding committees, please don't 'keep your views to yourself unless challenged'. All I know is Mrs Bear is a jolly good sort, trying to do what may be a jolly good work. What I want to know is: 1) Whether there is anything really worth saving? 2) Whether it can be pulled through? Don't be shy of saying the wrong thing. If you get a chance, draw her out. If you can make up your mind re. 1) and 2) I should like to know how it strikes you. I'd play the committee on her if you can – by all means. I truly agree 'Everybody hates 'em': why should a superior person like me be held to explain to a lot of common folk?' – Your suggestion that 'everlasting habitations' = permanent, is good, very good and new to me.

Hello! What's all this about predestination. What did I say? 'Refuse to believe in it?' – it's the only thing I can see left to believe in. There is nothing the human mind (*naturaliter Christiana*) needs to reflect on more than how a Divine purpose can understand and overrule the human. Don't start off on Hitler – because we just do not know. Try Sennacherib (Isaiah, 10 etc.), Jerusalem and Babylon, then St Luke – 21 especially vv. 25 and 28, then go on to the Fall of Rome in the Apocalypse.

God as a competent author.[1] As I see it, you (not me this time for I am a most *in*competent writer) start a book as you see it. In the middle, God gets in, says 'that's not what they'll do but this'. Not the characters interfering with the author (*a façon de parler*) but God – and he does this in a book and in the S.S.M.

    Yours sincerely in Christ
    Herbert Kelly S.S.M.

---

[1] Presumably this is continuing a discussion in a previous conversation which has not survived. It seems to pick up the theme of the creative Idea again.

Letter 15
HK to DLS

The Nursing Community
of Christ the Consoler
St George's House
6 North Hill
Highgate N6

[April 1938]

Dear Miss Sayers

Here is one more slip. I offered Mother Jessie for your contemplation as an attraction. Alas – she has gone to Truro. But the sisters are here. We are offered tea in the Mother's room. Then we can migrate to my prophetic chamber for cigs...

BUT: if you like studying Sisters, would you like to have tea with them, and then come up here. They are nice creatures. They know (a) your books; (b) your plays; (c) your *Sunday Times* letters.[1] It would please them I know/am sure. There is no reason you should the choice is – tea and a sisters' refectory or sherry in a bar?[2]

CODE: if you like the idea, please phone: 'Good idea'. I will understand and arrange. If I don't hear I'll let them know we will take tea in Mother's room. OR you can phone 'Better stick to arrangement', then the same.

Yours sincerely in Christ
Herbert Kelly S.S.M

---

[1] DLS wrote a series of articles for the *Sunday Times* in the later 1930s.
[2] It seems the alternatives offered are: tea in the superior's room with the community, followed by cigarettes in HK's room, or tea and supper in the sisters' dining room followed by a visit to a bar afterwards. HK's instructions seem very muddled. It is unclear what the outcome was and he continues to offer the visit in the following letter, almost as if he has forgotten his previous description of it.

Letter 16   St George's
HK to DLS   6 North Hill
                                                            Highgate

Palm Sunday

My dear Miss Sayers,

How is the play? I hope it has started to your satisfaction.

Please allow me: 1) to give you my hearty congratulations on your *Sunday Times* article which was really good.[1] It is just what I wanted you to do. 2) I think I told you I was going to be in London, and I am here till Easter Tuesday. Tuesday – the rest of Easter week I shall be with Lady Long @ Fulham.[2]

Do you yearn for 'Contacts'? This place is a Nursing Sisterhood (small) started by Mother Jessie, who was for some years Mother Superior of Truro.[3] She is a dear old lady of 79. Incidentally she is a 'Scott' – i.e. of the Buccleugh [sic] family, i.e. of the Queen.[4] So I learnt from my sister (not Lady Long) who was at Truro.[5] I learnt the family name from the Free Library folk who entered her as *Mrs* Scott! 'Mother' is deceptive to the ratepayers.

If you would care to see her in London, she would like to meet you, and I will arrange it. Tea 4 p.m. approx. We are about 250 yards from the number 11 tram terminus which runs past Highgate Tube Station.

If you are not in London this week or if you have no burnin' desire to see 'Mrs Scott/Mother Jessie' I expect to be at Fulham from Tuesday of Easter Week. Lady Long has asked me to go with her to see *THE* play – Wednesday afternoon. I have not heard but I presume the seats are already booked.

Don't you bother to go tubing about London – if you are not up to it. I rather fancy you'll be at home Holy Week. I wonder how you got on with Mrs Bear and the Committee.

If you'd prefer contact with Tubby Clayton (TOC H), I might see him next week. Doubt if I shall. I get very lazy, but he wrote me a delightful letter.

>Yours Sincerely in Christ
>Herbert Kelly S.S.M

[1] Probably, 'The Greatest Drama Ever Staged is the Official Creed of Christendom', *The Sunday Times*, 3 April 1938. This was subsequently published as a pamphlet.

[2] See Letter 5 above.

[3] The Community of the Epiphany, founded in 1883, which HK's sister, Edith Mary, entered c.1919. She was at their mission in Japan until 1928. See Anson, *Call of the Cloister*, pp.457–8. Mother Jessie (see above) was a member of the community.

[4] Probably Buccleuch. An ancient Scottish family connected with the Dukedom of Queensbury.

[5] i.e. Sister Edith Kelly.

Letter 17   [24 Newland Street
DLS to HK   Witham
                                   Essex]

18 April 1938

Dear Father Kelly,

Thank you so much for your letter: I hoped to be able to find time last week to run up to Highgate, but for one reason or another, I seem to be engaged every day until my return here. We had a little trouble in the angelic host owing to the departure of two Gabriels one after the other with some kind of internal disorder, and one way and another I could not get free. I hope, however, to be at the Theatre on Wednesday afternoon and to see you and Lady Long there.

Mrs. Bear was very kind to me on Palm Sunday, and I hope they were more or less entertained by what I had to say: at any rate, I know several of them came and saw the show. It would, indeed, be interesting if you could establish contact with Mr. Clayton, but I expect he is very busy.

Looking forward to seeing you again,

Yours very sincerely

[DLS]

Letter 18   Society of the Sacred Mission
HK to DLS   Kelham Theological College

21 April 1938

Dear Miss Sayers,

1) If by any chance you want to see me, I shall be at Holy Trinity, Charlton Lane, S.E.7 till Saturday week (i.e. from Monday – here, then 97 Hurlingham Court S.W.6 from 6 Feb.

2) Re. Play. It was *very* fine – the angels were gorgeous. Wish I could have heard better.[1]

3) I have just written to Clayton (enclosing a copy) and told him to write to you. Maybe, he will, but you know what male beings are (see Lady Ursula) – so if he doesn't, take a chance of your own – my advice.

Don't bother to return, nor to answer.

Yours sincerely in Christ

Herbert Kelly

---

[1] HK had hearing difficulties since youth. See Introduction.

Letter 19   [24 Newland Street
DLS to HK   Witham
                                                        Essex]

1 May 1938

Dear Father Kelly,

I feel very discourteous at not having replied to your letter or
come to see you, but last week was one prolonged and purgatorial
agitation. We were reduced to desperation by the fact that although the business for *Zeal* was building at the Westminster, we
could not carry on there, and could see no prospect either of
transferring or of raising money to finance a tour. In this hopeless
situation we implored God for a miracle, to which he responded
with His accustomed sense of humour by arousing the interest of
the hardest headed and the hardest hearted management in town!
We had nearly a week of frantic negotiations, during which they
wanted first to make all the cast play for a pittance, secondly to cut
down half the cast, and thirdly to make the author work for
nothing. After agitated bargaining on all these points, we at last
succeeded in screwing out of them mean, though just barely
adequate, terms and this Shylock bargain was finally clinched at
midnight on Friday. The result is that the play reopens at the
Garrick Theatre on Tuesday week, May 10th. Amid all the whirling
of the dust of conflict, I fear I quite lost touch with my friends and
my correspondence; I hope you will forgive me.

I am so glad you liked the play; I am immensely pleased with
the production and the acting that my company has given me. I
have not yet heard from Mr Clayton, but as soon as I am in a more
coherent frame of my mind, I will write to him.

With very many thanks,
        Yours sincerely.
            [Dorothy L. Sayers]

Letter 20   House of Epiphany
HK to DLS   Truro, Cornwall
                                                 6 May 1938

Dear Miss Sayers

Warm congratulations. I wonder whether it would make a talkie film. I doubt it. Its power lies in its significance rather than incident, and as a spectacle it wants its colour. I hope it will run long. Certainly should do.

I have finished and am off via Liverpool tomorrow and back to Kelham by Friday next.

I have read two books on the Inquisition whence divers useful notes. It is, to me, a profoundly interesting subject – psychologically, morally. I have also done – nearly done – some notes on modern physical theories.

N.B. I heard from someone in London that you 'will soon become a member of the R.C. community'. Information about one's own future is at once so interesting and so hard to come by that I should be wanting in friendliness if I did not give you what there is available. I thought you might be interested to know.

Your theatre manager makes me sad – also mad. This community has a branch in Japan, so I have been trying to learn more about the beloved country. That too is frightening. I can go on reading Psalms. The psalmists understand everything – just because they have the courage to face what is so perplexing and horrible – the power and success of the proud – just on the line of the Inquisition. If I did not believe in God what is there? Madness? – I'm not [mad]; suicide? – I have not the courage; cynicism? – the wickedest of all this lot to my mind.

Please don't apologise for being busy. Is the new ribbon to celebrate the Garrick? You see, I have learnt to notice.

                    Yours sincerely in Christ
                       Herbert Kelly S.S.M

Letter 21   [24 Newland Street
DLS to HK   Witham
                                              Essex]

16 May 1938

Dear Father Kelly,

Many thanks for your letter. We are hoping to do well with
the show at the Garrick, though, of course, it will again take a little
time to build up business. I should be rather afraid of what the
films might do with it; I fear the theology would be likely to suffer!

I am exceedingly interested to learn that I am about to join the
Roman Catholic Church; if your informant had heard the things I
said about that institution the other day (stimulated by Douglas
Woodruff's disagreeable criticism of *Zeal* in *Punch*) he might
reconsider his prophecy.[1] There are moments when I feel that the
Inquisition was one of the least dishonest of its activities.

I went to see Tubby Clayton the other day, who was very
agreeable though somewhat preoccupied; he seems to have got
into a curious habit of saying: 'Good, good; well done!' at intervals
throughout the conversation, with curiously little relevance to the
context. It must come of having so much to do with Boy Scouts
and Leagues of Youth. However, I was inveigled by one of his
young men into promising to go and talk about Religious Drama
to Toc H, on the understanding, of course, that they would give
me publicity for *Zeal*. I get to feel more and more like the unjust
steward every day. I ought to be getting on with my new novel,[2]
instead I am impelled to write a play about Herod the Great;[3] it
will probably turn out to be another version of the downfall of the
proud.

    With all good wishes,
        Yours sincerely,
            Dorothy L. Sayers

[1] Douglas Woodruff, 1897–1978, was editor of the Catholic magazine *The Tablet* from 1936 to 1947. His letter, 6 April 1938, to the editor of *Punch* was critical of the play.

[2] 'Thrones, Dominations'. DLS began writing this novel, the latest in her series of Lord Peter Wimsey/Harriet Vane books, in the mid-1930s but it was never finished. Her dramatic and theological work took precedence. The novel remained in fragments until it was completed and published in 1998 by Jill Paton Walsh. The title is taken from John Milton's *Paradise Lost* and refers to two of the angelic categories, suggesting that angels were still very much on her mind at this time. Dorothy L. Sayers and Jill Paton Walsh, *Thrones, Dominations* (London: Hodder Paperbacks, 1998.

[3] Only the first act of this play was written (or survived). It is in manuscript form at the Marion E. Wade Center, Wheaton College, Illinois.

Letter 22   Society of the Sacred Mission
HK to DLS   Kelham Theological College

21 May 1938

Dear Miss Sayers

Curiouser and curiouser. Is this telepathy? Re. you and Rome (N.B. it was not all *my* idea I had memories of Sheila K Smith[1] – never read her – probably couldn't – but you are much too theological to be R.C.). I had just got back when your letter arrived with its reference to *Punch*, also the Inquisition. Must be telepathy.

Before the holidays, I had read that old atheist McCabe (ex-Franciscan)[2] who had a good deal to say about the R.C. Literature Committee and its borrowings [sic] with a reference to Poynter – *Rome at Close Quarters*.[3] I am trying to get it. Poynter was on it.[4]

The Inquisition is also an old friend of mine. Studied it carefully in Lea's *History*.[5] Wrote a long analysis lecture on it for these boys.[6] But during the holidays I found two new books and got a lot of new quotes. It's not the cruelty of it which shocks me

– Bolsheviks, Nazis, Fascists can all parallel that. It is the blasphemy of its explanations etc.

When I got back, I picked up some old *Punches* in the Common Room and spotted that review. *Punch* has been very much at R.C. disposal ever since Burnand.[7] Of course I had no guess at the name [of Douglas Woodruff]. Don't know him. Now you tell me who he is.

How funny it all is. You have no idea of how little I know of people and who they are. I have just read very carefully your very excellent article in *St Martin's Review*[8] and carried on my eyes to the art of Dick Sheppard by Middleton Murry (know the name but can't remember what for).[9] Dick Shepherd – I never did like. Thought him seeking cheap publicity value. But Middleton Murry's remarks on 'The Church' and its value to Shepherd (all the more so because D.S. didn't recognise it) are simply priceless.

It is 11.45 a.m. and I am still in bed. I shall get up in an hour or so. At seventy-eight (nearly) my head is crowded with new ideas, and I have neither time nor energy to do anything with them, I am rather amused at it really.

Well, thank you for writing. It is nice to hear from people who can do things. Herod was afraid of God. Dictators always are.

> Yours most sincerely in Christ
> [H Kelly]

---

[1] Sheila Kaye-Smith, 1887–1956, English author who became a Roman Catholic in 1929.

[2] Joseph McCabe, 1867–1955, a Roman Catholic Franciscan priest who left his Order and the Church in 1896. He wrote and lectured widely on free-thinking.

[3] J.W. Poynter, *Rome at Close Quarters*, first published in 1931.

[4] This paragraph is an example of HK's epistolary style later in life. His active mind is running over a number of thoughts with which his reader will struggle to connect.

[5] Henry Charles Lea, *A History of the Inquisition of the Middle Ages,* published in three volumes from 1887. Notes made by HK on the Inquisition are preserved in the archive (SSM/HK/RN/B/12).

[6] HK's talks on Church History, in four volumes, form part of his lecture series. The fourth volume ends with the Crusades so possibly a fifth volume covering

the Inquisition was made but has not survived. Much of his theological thinking over the years emerged in his Church History lectures and he was urged to publish the series. It was turned down by SPCK in 1928 (SSM/HL/L/715A and 725).

[7] Francis Cowley Burnand, 1836–1917, was editor of *Punch* from 1880–1896.

[8] No journal of this name can be identified for the period.

[9] Dick Sheppard, 1880–1937, an Anglican priest. He had been dean of Canterbury Cathedral, 1929–1931, and was a Christian pacifist. John Middleton Murry, 1889–1957, was an editor, author and critic. He is perhaps best remembered today for his friendship with D. H. Lawrence, support for T.S. Eliot, and marriage to Katherine Mansfield. He published many of the 'Bloomsbury' authors in the early twentieth century. He was for many years a supporter of the Christian pacifist movement.

Letter 23   [24 Newland Street
DLS to HK   Witham
                                                                    Essex]

24 May 1938[1]

Dear Father Kelly,

Douglas Woodruff is the editor of *The Tablet* (which also launched a contemptuous dig at *Zeal*). Having readily detected the grinding of the Roman axe behind the grin of the Roman wolf, I wrote to him, saying that I did not mind his crabbing the show, but I did object to his sheltering behind the skirts of the Establishment and rebuking me under the cover of the 'High Church Divines'. I further (just to annoy him) accused him of Docetism[2] and of confounding the Persons of the Blessed Trinity. He replied in two rather ill-argued letters. In the first, he said he thought William's speech to Michael might lead people to suppose that the Church had done a certain amount of 'botching and altering' since Christ departed and left them to it. I avoided this trap (though one might adduce arguments in favour of such a proposition) and merely replied that the whole point of Michael's reply and of the play was that the Master Architect might safely 'leave the work to others', with the assistance of the Holy Ghost, and that, as a matter of historical fact, there had been no 'botching', even at Canterbury. From his second letter I rather gathered that, while willing to allow Christ the experience of a few minor pains and inconveniences incidental to humanity, he boggled at supposing Him really to have been ground in such a mill of spiritual suffering as one might infer from the *lama sabachthani*: token payments, by all means, but not the whole debt. That seemed to me to be what the Red Queen would call 'a poor, thin way of doing things' and I really began to wonder whether he had ever thought of Jesus as a real live *person* at all. However, it was all getting very difficult and metaphysical so I left it there, having at any rate succeeded in making him apologise for the sneering tone of his review.

John Middleton Murry is an author and critic, editor of *The Athenaeum* for some time after the war. He has written a number of books, including a *Life of Christ* (which is probably what you connect him with – I should think it would be awful):[3] according to Frank Swinnerton,[4] he 'turned first Christian and then Christian Communist', whatever that means exactly. He was the husband of Katherine Mansfield[5] and a friend of D. H. Lawrence (at least, until Lawrence took to calling him 'Judas', having indeed every reason to cry 'save me from my friends!') and wrote a very emotional sort of biography of him, called *Son of Woman*.[6] I should think he was probably quite right about Dick Sheppard. I only met D.S. twice. He possessed an astonishing amount of personal charm, but he made me feel a little uncomfortable. I think he was sincere, but he seemed to me over-anxious for the affection of all and sundry. He impressed me as being quite restless, feverish and essentially unhappy, always in quest of reassurance and, I am sure, lacking in intellect – but then I always tend to rate intellect too high and to be embarrassed by magnetic personality and that kind of thing.

Herod (confound him) is becoming very insistent, trampling ferociously in my mind over the heads of all the other things it is my duty to do. Can you or any of your brethren guide me to a book (not too learned and difficult) about the position of the Jews under the Roman Empire, between Maccabees and St Matthew? I want to know how they carried on their daily life and institutions under that alien but tolerant despotism. Herod seems to have had a bad time with them, because, though he got back Jerusalem from the Parthians and rebuilt the Temple and did quite a lot of the enlightened monarch business, they hated and despised him for being Rome's nominee, and for building a wicked heathen amphitheatre, and especially for being a Philistine and not 'hundred-percent Jewish (thus the 'whirligig of time brings in its revenges!').[7] I expect he had it pretty well dinned into his ears about the expected 'pure-Jewish' Messiah and the 'pure Jewish' kingdom-to-be, and all the rest of it – his wife's family apparently lost no opportunity of rubbing it in about his low antecedents. I don't wonder that, after a long lifetime of disappointment in his own offspring he lost his (always very precarious) hold on his own temper and determined to do away with Messianic pretenders. I can see the development of his character very clearly, but where I'm stuck is on domestic and political details – what sort of people he would have had in his household, how far he could administer the province off his own bat and how much he had to act for Rome, what were the relations between the Jewish Church and the Roman State, and so forth. I am extremely ignorant of the history of that – and indeed of any – period. I imagine that to Rome he would appear very oriental and barbaric and to the Jews sadly occidental and internationalised – rather like an Indian maharajah who has been educated at Oxford, neither flesh, fowl nor good red herring.

I too, you see, am bursting over with ideas, and seem to have no time to deal with them. But it's great fun. It would be awful to come to the end of one's ideas. Good luck to the Inquisition. As to blasphemy – the R.C.'s seem to me to specialise in blasphemous explanations. Some well-wisher (anxious to keep me out of the Roman fold) favoured me with a revolting little pamphlet on Purgatory, which I shouldn't have thought anybody would have the face to publish at this time of day. Anyway, the Vatican seems to be in rather bad odour today, even among its own people, for its political dishonesty and the pruriency of its sexual ethics. R.C. theology seems to me to be chiefly dialectics – though I suppose some of the really important writers attach meaning to the terms they bandy about so freely – even if Douglas Woodruff doesn't!

Lord! What a long letter to bore you with –

Very sincerely yours

[DLS]

---

[1] NB The first page of this letter is not reproduced in the Barbara Reynolds edition which begins with: 'John Middleton Murry…' *Letters, Vol II*, p.80.

[2] The disputed doctrine that Christ did not have a real or human body but was merely a phantom or spirit.

[3] John Middleton Murry, *Life of Jesus Christ* (London: J Cape, 1926).

[4] Frank Arthur Swinnerton, 1884–1982, novelist, critic, biographer and essayist.

[5] Her second husband, she married him in 1918.

[6] John Middleton Murry, *Son of Woman: The Story of D.H. Lawrence* (London: J Cape and H Smith, 1931).

[7] *Twelfth Night*, Act 5, Scene 1.

Letter 24   House of the Sacred Mission
HK to DLS   Kelham

[postcard 24 May 1938]

To redeem error. Did you get my letter? Were you interested in Poynter?[1] I've just seen it. Conclusion: don't be interested! Very poor book. No information of value.

Herbert Kelly, SSM

[1] See Letter 22.

Letter 25
DLS to HK

[24 Newland Street
Witham
Essex]

4 July 1938

Dear Father Kelly,

Many thanks for your letter. The *Zeal of Thy House* unfortunately was not able to survive the double removal, first from the Westminster and then from the Garrick, and finished its London run last Saturday. We are hoping to get a tour out in September, and should hope, in the ordinary course of events, to go to Nottingham.[1] Under these circumstances, I do not quite know what to say about an amateur performance at Newark. I am passing your letter on to my agent, who will be able to decide whether such a performance is advisable as things stand. [2]

There wasn't really anything in my letter that really needed answering, except that I inquired for books about the period of Herod the Great, but Professor Eileen Power and Father Hood of the Pusey House have already kindly directed me to various sources of information.[3]

With kindest regards and best wishes

[DLS]

[1] The provincial tour opened in Norwich in October 1938. DLS, unable to get financial backers for it, invested her own savings and raised further funds by returning to her old craft and writing advertising copy for Horlicks. The run

was not successful and DLS lost money although she enjoyed the tour, travelling with the production from venue to venue.

[2] Kelly's letter has not survived but it must have contained a request for an amateur performance of *Zeal* at Kelham. DLS wrote to her literary agent, Margery Vosper, on 4 July 1938: 'I enclose copies of two letters which have come in about amateur performances. Father Kelly's application for the theological students is in a rather different category from the ordinary amateur show, and it might be possible to give him permission for what he wants, if you thought well. In any case, please treat him with peculiar tenderness, as he is some fantastic age, 84 or something!' Reynolds, *Letters Vol II*, p.85. (HK was seventy-eight in 1938).

[3] Eileen Power, 1889–1940, economic historian and medievalist. Lecturer at Girton College, Cambridge and, later, London School of Economics by this time she had retired. Archibald Frederic Hood, 1895–1975, was Principal of Pusey House, Oxford between 1934 and 1952.

Letter 26   St George's House
HK to DLS   6 North Hill
                                                      Highgate N6

Xmas Day 1938

Dear Miss Sayers

Thanks for your Xmas card. I am always so ashamed, because I never have any, and never remember to send to all the nice people who remember me. But I don't forget them all the same.

I am coming up to London from 28 December until 5 January. I shall be at 57 Hurlingham Court, Putney Bridge with Lady Long. I am sure she would like to see you. From 5 to 9 January I shall be with my pet sisterhood (nurses) at 6 North Hill, Highgate. (Take bus no. 9 to Highgate Station and then the no. 11 tram to North Hill which starts from the terminus. 6 North Hill is about 350 yards on the right-hand side, just below a little Post Office).

This is as bad as forgetting Xmas. But it is an intimation of friendship. It would be a pleasure to meet. I wonder (1) whether you are going to be in London. Wonder (2) whether you are yearin' to talk theology. Wonder (3) whether you would like to see Lady Long OR Mother Jessie, formerly Mother of Truro (now a sister of Truro and Mother of the Nursing community – Mrs Scott to the ratepayers).

Don't you bother if you're busy or not feelin' like it. Only please accept this as an apology for the Xmas card that didn't arrive.

   Yours sincerely in Christ

    [HK]

Letter 27   [24 Newland Street

DLS to HK   Witham

                  Essex]

20 February 1939

Dear Father Kelly,

Forgive my delay in replying to your letter; I have been furiously at work trying to get my new play about Faustus finished for Canterbury.[1] I have sent a line to Mr. Tompkins saying that I will read through his book with pleasure and try and give him my opinion upon it for what it is worth.[2]

  With all best wishes,

    Yours sincerely,

     [DLS]

---

[1] *The Devil to Pay* was an interpretation of the Faustus legend and presented a modern perspective of the problem of evil as the rejection of responsibility and retreat into infantilism. It was presented at the Canterbury Festival in June 1939 with Harcourt Williams in the role of Faustus. It was transferred to the Haymarket Theatre, London, in August 1939 bur received poor reviews (although T.S. Eliot appears to have liked it, Reynolds, *Letters Vol II*, p. 134). It

was taken off after war was declared the following month and has never been performed since (see Barbara Reynolds, *Dorothy L. Sayers: Her Life and Soul* (London: Sceptre Books, 1998) pp. 329–3.
[2] Mr Tompkins cannot be traced. Neither his letter nor details of his proposed book have survived.

Letter 28   Society of the Sacred Mission
HK to DLS   Kelham Theological College

10 March 1939

My dear Miss Sayers,

   Here's a funny go. Just got the enclosed from one of my S.C.M. friends.[1] Silly! I calls it. Reminds me of people asking somebody to plead with the publishers on their behalf. I expect you get stacks of letters asking you to do so. Three people – one time or another – have done that for me unasked – and the publisher turned me down every time.

   However, I expect you know all about Oldham and the Oxford Conference, and I know you know the S.C.M. I haven't seen Oldham for donkey's years – 1910 more or less.[2] I told them to blaze away. I hope to be up in Highgate in Holy Week.

           Yours sincerely in Christ
               [HK]

[1] This may refer to the request from Mr Tompkins, see Letter 27 above.
[2] Joseph Oldham, 1874–1969, was a missionary in India for many years. He was never ordained. He and HK had corresponded in 1908 concerning the World Missionary Conference which was to be held in 1910. He was involved in the Christian ecumenism movement and in 1937 organised the Oxford Conference on 'Church, Community and State'. The conference looked at the causes of the rise in totalitarian regimes, especially in Germany and condemned the 'secularist revolt' and subsequent birth of materialist 'cults', John Carter Wood, 'Going

"part of the way together": Christian intellectuals, modernity and the secular in 1930s and 1940s Britain', *Contemporary British History*, 34, 2020, pp. 580–602, especially p. 585. Presumably Mr Tompkins' book dealt with the matter. HK was already involved with the Oxford Group Movement (see SSM/HK/SP/17) and his initial mention of Oldham led to DLS's subsequent correspondence with him about a weekly Christian newsletter (see Reynolds, *Dorothy L. Sayers*, p. 376ff. For DLS's correspondence with Oldham see also Reynolds, *Letters, Vol II*, p. 133–34, 136–8 and 165–6. HK's series of articles on the Oxford Group, 'The Group', *The SSM Quarterly* for 1933 received considerable interest (SSM/S/QP/8).

Letter 29	House of the Sacred Mission
HK to DLS	Kelham

11 June 1939

Dear Miss Sayers,

There is a muddle going. If I get on the wrong horse, you will excuse me. But a young man of ours drifts in with a vague message from a vague 'somebody' in Nottingham that you are going to be there on the 26th of this month, with your play – presumably *Zeal*, and would Father Alfred Kelly like a ticket. Confusion so confounded that I doubt everything.

Firstly Fr Alfred K. is (a) a distinguished local tennis player and (b) preacher. Quite probably, better known locally, but he is my brother, not ME. So, we suppose it means me. Secondly, is it true that you and the Company are coming to Nottingham on June 26th?

If so, then, alas, I am getting too feeble to go anywhere – much as I should like to see you and it again. *Per contra*, we have connections with Nottingham. We have a parish there (by the mainline station).[1] Also, Bishop Talbot (of St Mary's, Nottingham) is a very dear friend of mine.[2] Further, Walker of Averham is our rector and very keen on plays etc. If you can let me have four bills, I will try to get them interested.

But if you are to be there, I wonder if I could tempt you over to see us. In some ways it is rather poor doings. We used to have a 'Visitors' Room', but it has all been smashed up – the very bricks broken into bits, because we are building over it, but you can see our truly wonderful chapel – most wonderful as ever was! We could give you tea in your chariot, in the village, or at the Rectory. On the whole, if you have a passion for architecture, the chapel is worth a journey. Otherwise, I do not think it is.

High Mass in the Great Chapel, Kelham

But while I am writing, I just mention, that I shall be at Highgate sometime in August, also at Fulham (Putney Bridge), I only mention it because I think it is also possible that I may never be in London again! Life out of bed is hardly worth living.

Nor is this letter of any assured value, except that if there is a message from you which has got a bit mixed, I should not like it ignored.

   Yours very sincerely in Christ

   [HK]

[1] This was St George's, which was run by SSM from 1911–1974.

[2] Neville Stuart Talbot, 1879–1943, son of 'old bishop Talbot' mentioned in Letter 3. He was bishop of Pretoria, assistant bishop of Southwell and vicar of St Mary's, Nottingham. DLS was in correspondence with Talbot on 25 January 1939 and 7 March 1939 (Reynolds, *Letters, Vol II*, pp. 116–8).

Letter 30   As from The White House,
DLS to HK   St Peter's Lane,
                                         Canterbury.

15 June 1939

Dear Father Kelly,

I think there is a muddle. I am coming to Nottingham on the 26th, but not with *The Zeal of Thy House*, which has just finished its tour, but merely to talk at Bishop Talbot's instigation to 'Youth' and on the 27th to a bunch of clergymen. If I am able to find time on the morning of the 27th to run over to Kelham, I should love to do so. I will, if I may, let you know nearer the time when I get back to town as I am at present here dealing with my new Canterbury play, *The Devil to Pay*, which is starting on Saturday. I enclose a copy of it, which may amuse you, though some of its theology is, perhaps, a little imaginative.

With best wishes

Yours very sincerely

[DLS]

Letter 31   House of the Sacred Mission
HK to DLS   Kelham

22 June 1939

Dear Miss Sayers

I ought to have written before to thank you for your book
which intrigued me vastly. [1] It wants a lot of thinking over; the main
outstanding points are wholly right – to my mind. I haven't it by
me now for the little bees are swarming – not round but actually in
the pot – very greedily. Now – oh *where's* that letter? 26th did you
say? That is Monday. Well, we shall be more or less free and glad
to see you. We have tea at 3.30 rather a muddled time for you I
expect. 1.30 – 3 they are out on the cricket field, except those on
jobs. There is a free road through for visitors. If you can make it
round then abouts I will have something for you in your car – if
you come that fashion. It would be nice if you could bring Bishop
Neville Talbot over.

I have a lecture between 4.10 and 5.15 or so, otherwise I am
free all times. Of course, anytime I will put you in the chapel – you
can also gaze at the new buildings.

Give my best love to the Bishop, he's a very dear friend of
mine – for the last thirty years or more   - even though he does
NOT come to see me. That's the habit folks get into.

Yours sincerely in Christ
[HK]

PS. Your last note said you were getting it 'finished'. The whole
sorrow of life is its fleeting joys, the mere joy it offers of being able
to say 'finished'. Just one squeak, then you start on something else.
I seldom get that far.

---

[1] Presumably *The Devil to Pay* which was first performed in June 1939.

Letter 32
Secretary to DLS

22 June 1939

Drear Father Kelly

Miss Dorothy L. Sayers has asked me to write and tell you that she is afraid she will not have time to come over to see you when she is in Nottingham next week: she will have to get back to London as soon as possible, as she is extremely busy just now. She hopes to have her new play, *The Devil to Pay*, produced at His Majesty's Theatre about the 8th August.

      Yours very truly
        [Secretary]

Letter 33   [24 Newland Street
DLS to HK   Witham
                                    Essex]

2 July 1939

Dear Father Kelly,

I was so terribly sorry not to have been able to come and see you after all at Nottingham: it was really a great disappointment, but as I think my secretary explained to you, I was thrown into a great turmoil of business over the arrangements to produce *The Devil to Pay* in London, and could only dash up to Nottingham, speak my speeches and hurry back by the next train. I hope very much that I shall, before long, be able to visit Kelham.

I am glad you found *The Devil to Pay* interesting, and could approve of it on main lines; its theology is, of course, not so straightforward as *Zeal*: in fact it is, perhaps, a little obscure in places, and this, I think, has been an advantage to it with the Press, who always treat obscurity with respect. It has irritated the *New English Weekly*, who, having no good answer themselves to the problem of evil, very much dislike anyone else's attempt to find one.[1] The entertaining thing is, the number of people who think it would be so nice to be turned into a little innocent dog, and do not see they are exactly the people against whom the play conveys a warning.[2] Anyway, I hope we may do well with it in town, though I fear we would have more chance with it if it would please God to call Adolf Hitler to Himself; perhaps He does not want him!

With best wishes and again very, very many regrets that I was not able to accept your invitation.

Yours very sincerely

[DLS]

---

[1] *New English Weekly*, a journal first published in 1932. It was a review of 'Public affairs, literature and the arts'. Contributors included T.S Eliot and George Orwell.

[2] In the play the soul of Faustus is found to have become a black dog, with a real dog appearing on stage (see Reynolds, *Dorothy L. Sayers*, p. 330).

Letter 34   [House of the Sacred Mission
HK to DLS   Kelham]

6 July 1939

Dear Miss Sayers

Thank you so much for your kind letter, I quite understand, do come if you get a chance.

I hope – expect – mean – to be in London for the mid-fortnight of August (as the good lady said: 'D.V.' – for one week).

I don't think I know the *New English Weekly*. I can quite believe it: if you will go asking questions about the very root of problems, there are two sets of people (a) those who make their living out of a conventional answer; (b) those who make a living by deriding that answer. The former (a) will be puzzled; (b) will be very cross at your suggesting the problem is still there. This very afternoon as ever is, I have a lecture on 'the future state', with those beauty-fully mapped out divisions of Paradise, Purgatory and Hell.

N.B while on the subject, do you know C.C.J. Webb – the best of Oxford Christian philosophers – who derides the 'continued existence theories' as un-Christian.[1]

N.B Karl Barth's son is here – sampling varied theologies.[2]

Poor old Hitler – did you ever see a face so strikingly unhappy – miserable.

I should like to write an article on the history of 'Tragedies', the Middle Ages, for example, are full of tragedies and of failures – men knew they failed. The Crusaders; the Papacy (from Hildebrand to Boniface VIII down to Borgia et al.); St Francis, St Bernard, St Louis, Savonarola and St Thomas Aquinas. Then from the Renaissance on to the tragedies of men who thought they suc-ceeded: Luther and Loyola, Wesley and Ligouri. But there are still sprinklings of tragedy in the old style; Cromwell, Laud, Napoleon, Newman, and then, what seem to us confusions, beginning with Wilson, because we are waiting for the end.[3]

As to Hitler, I do not ask to get him out to make way for Goebbels and Goring.

Goodnight, it is 1.50 p.m. and I am going to sleep! – In preparation for a discussion on the 'indeterminate state' – most appropriate!!

Yours sincerely in Christ

[HK]

---

[1] Clement Charles Julian Webb, 1865–1954, Magdalene and, later, Oriel colleges, Oxford. A critic of sociological theories that treated religion as only a

social phenomenon (e.g. Émile Durkheim). In *God and Personality* (1918) and *Divine Personality and Human Life* (1920) he explored the relationship between divine personality and man's social, political and religious activities.

[2] Marcus Barth, 1915–1994. There is little detail in the archives of Barth junior's stay. Dewey in 'SSM Chronicle' notes merely that Marcus Barth 'visited Kelham in 1939 and talked with Kelly. What seemed to impress the young theologian most were two items of decoration in HK's study: a picture of a pig (in which Kelly saw the glory of God and the Resurrection) and an 'L' plate (which he kept to remind himself that he was a permanent novice), p.194.

[3] It is not clear to whom he is referring here: possibly U.S. president, Thomas Woodrow Wilson, 1856–1924.

Letter 35   24 Newland St
DLS to HK   Witham
                                              Essex

19 September 1940

Dear Father Kelly

Thank you so much for your kind and interesting letter.[1] I had been wondering how you were getting along and trying to settle down to write to you. I find the times unsettling; one is perpetually waiting for something to happen, and I am apt to be lazy and disintegrated and fall back to knitting socks for sailors instead of getting on with things. I am so sorry I missed you in Town. I haven't had very much to take me there since the Blitzkrieg started, and since the bombs began to fall I have pusillanimously stayed at home. The last time I went up it was to a meeting of clerics and laity at the BBC who were trying to work out plans for some sort of 'call to religion' with musical and dramatic accompaniments.[2] I found it rather depressing, because the wretched pacifist question boiled up at once, and these people always contrive to put one into an awkward position, as though one was completely corrupted by Caesar, while sitting loftily on the Mount with Christ and Mr

Gandhi. And the clergy who were not pacifist, but showed a great reluctance to fight the issue, all seemed disposed to believe that it was a chief business of the Church to advocate Socialism and economic reform. So easy to say, 'let's have the simple Gospel, and consider what Christ would have done'. But what is the 'simple Gospel'? And whatever Christ 'would have done', there's one thing he resolutely refused to do: viz to sit on committees and argue about politics. I don't know how it is, but convocations of the Godly always give one the feeling that everything is doomed to destruction and that nothing is worth fighting for. *You* don't take that view, I notice. Perhaps the people who sit on BBC committees are the wrong kind of clergymen. They don't seem able to keep the Law and the Gospel distinct in their minds. And the Pacifists say: 'If we countenance any sort of war, we are at odds with Christ'. I said 'If it comes to that, we are always at odds with Christ, why pick on that one thing? If one is to stop preaching Christianity every time original sin involves us in a position that's at odds with Christ, the Church had better shut up shop'. I don't really see why it's any more anti-Gospel to go to war than to go to law; both things involve, ultimately, invoking force to restrict social offences, and neither proceeding is very charitable. But I don't suppose that even the most rigid pacifist obeys the instruction that if he does go to law and is called to pay damages, he will pay the damages twice over in accordance with Matthew V. 40.[3] And I bet they all insure their lives and property, lilies of the field or no lilies of the field. What really bothers them is the killing of the body —and here I sympathise with them, because I am a shocking coward and don't at all want to be killed, but I really can't pretend there's any moral superiority about disliking death. Anyhow, they all made me feel very gloomy, including the socialist parsons, who all seem to think that the difficulties of labour will be smoothed away by getting the wages right, never mind what happens to the work. I tried to suggest to them (along the lines of the little section on work in *Creed or Chaos?*) that it was necessary, along with the wages question, to get a right attitude to work.[4]

They thought this very moral and constructive – it didn't seem to have occurred to them before that it made any difference whether or not the worker was interested in beholding the result of the work – which shows how hopelessly we have got wound up into the 'economic theory' of society.

The other thing they all babbled about was European Federation. That worries me too, because the one Federation of Free Peoples that does exist and that seems to work pretty well – viz. the British Commonwealth – seems to be the one thing for which they have no sort of use. I'm getting more and more unregulated and inclined to the view that if somebody has got to be Caesar it may as well be us, because with all our faults we seem to be less anti-social and unpleasant than the rest, I don't see any point about busting up a thing that does work in favour of a European Federation which is no more likely to work than the League of Nations, or the temporal sovereignty of Rome. But I dare not say that kind of thing to Liberal clergymen.

I am not writing any detective stories at present. I can't be interested in one corpse under the sofa, when all these terrific events are going on, also, I've come to the conclusion that detective stories have rather a bad effect on people, because they encourage the belief that there is one nice, neat, simple, mechanical 'solution' to every problem and that they can somehow 'solve' human nature and social 'problems' by finding a trick of the machinery. I'm pretty sure that's the real reason for the extraordinary inter-war boom in detective fiction; it soothes the people by suggesting that everything can be seen in terms of problems with one watertight solution. And life isn't like that.

The only book I'm writing at the moment is an odd kind of thing called the *Mind of The Maker*,[5] all about the ways the Athanasian Formula works out in terms of creative art. It's really based on that speech of St Michael's at the end of *Zeal of Thy House*. When I get it done, I should like you to read it, if you can spare the time. People won't understand it, and will think it either silly or blasphemous, but it is a true record of experience so far as it goes.

I see that you are to be congratulated upon a recent birthday – please accept my best, though belated, wishes.[6] These are interesting times to live in, though terrifying. I have a feeling that the war is making us somehow rather less wicked or stupid than we were – if only we don't get too exhausted before the end comes.

Yours with affection and gratitude

Dorothy L. Sayers

[1] The letter referred to here appears to have been lost.

[2] In February 1940 DLS was invited to contribute to the BBC's war effort. This resulted in a series of plays for children entitled *The Man Born to be King*, broadcast in December 1941, which was to create much controversy (see Letter 38 below). The BBC involvement was more successful than her short-lived engagement with the Ministry of Information which also began at this time (and to which it seems she is referring here). The Ministry found her difficult to work with, and she described it as an 'overcrowded monkey house' (Reynolds, *Letters, Vol II*, p.137 and *Dorothy L. Sayers*, p. 334).

[3] Matthew chapter 5, verse 40; 'if a man takes you to law and would have your tunic, let him have your cloak as well'.

[4] DLS gave an address to the Church Tutorial Classes Association, Derby, on 4 May 1940 entitled 'Creed or Chaos?'. This was subsequently included in a collection of essays first published in 1947 and entitled *Creed or Chaos?* (Manchester, NH, Sophia Institute Press, 1974), pp. 27–54, for the section on work see pp. 51–3. It is here that she sets out her thoughts on a Christian doctrine of work.

[5] Sayers, *Mind of the Maker*, first published 1941 (London: Continuum, 1994).

[6] HK's eightieth birthday was on 18 July 1940. Dewey, 'SSM Chronicle', records that 'Fr Kelly kept his 80th birthday on July 18th. There was no special festivity such as marked the 70th and 75th anniversaries. So, he kept the day as a feria, with the usual daily routine: morning, lecture; after lunch, wood-cutting; after tea, writing; in the evening: a Dorothy Sayers [presumably one of her '"tec stories"]. But it is hoped that the passing of the war will enable his nine times nine to be suitably observed' (p. 198).

Letter 36   House of the Sacred Mission
HK to DLS   Kelham

10 October 1940

Dear Miss Sayers

One question is how soon to answer letters. If one answered
by return either that ends it, or it gets on to two a week. Well –
yours is dated 19 September this is 3 weeks.

'Waiting for somethin' to happen'. I am worse off than you
are because I have an extra war on. Japan's too far off while we're
watching a blitzkrieg of our own. But Japan is 'my' country. I spent
5–6 years there, and it is the only bit of my life I can bear to
remember. Well, the rest makes me sick and hot (except the
Student Movement lot and Swanwick maybe).[1] But Japan liked me.
The Missionary world there, English and American, was like a
teacup. All third-rate people doing the most vital epoch-making
work. So, a second-rater – same as me – was as big as a herring
among minnows. It was a funny business but gratifying to one's
self-importance and vanity. I was so hopeful, and now this.

What you call 'the BBC lot' I call 'the signpost lot'. I am utterly
with you. I want – maybe I shall – make a collection of 'wicked-
ness'. The worst I know calls itself 'Church Militant'.[2] Ever see it?
Maybe I'll get you one. Look at the blurb on the front page:
'Religious Hitlerism' I called it to the Archbishop of York and he
agreed. The only difference is that the pious assert themselves in
words – Hitler with tanks.

I want to (but certainly shan't) write another 'Gospel' book
called 'God and His World' along the lines of the collect for Trinity
VIII.[3]

While I so utterly agree with what you say in your previous
letter, may I criticise? (Don't like doing it, but also don't like you
saying 'Christ resolutely refused: to sit on committees' (He wasn't
asked) or to 'argue about politics' (He never argued about any-

thing). It is tricky. He did throw out big suggestive principles. But all this wants a lot of working out and thinking over.

As to pacifism. Do you ever ask them what they make of the Book of Revelation? Also, of the Fall of Jerusalem? Evidently in all these chapters they treat it as God's own work. And what about Isaiah 10 re. Sennacharib? Also, all the bits in Jeremiah and Daniel re. Nebuchadnezzar?

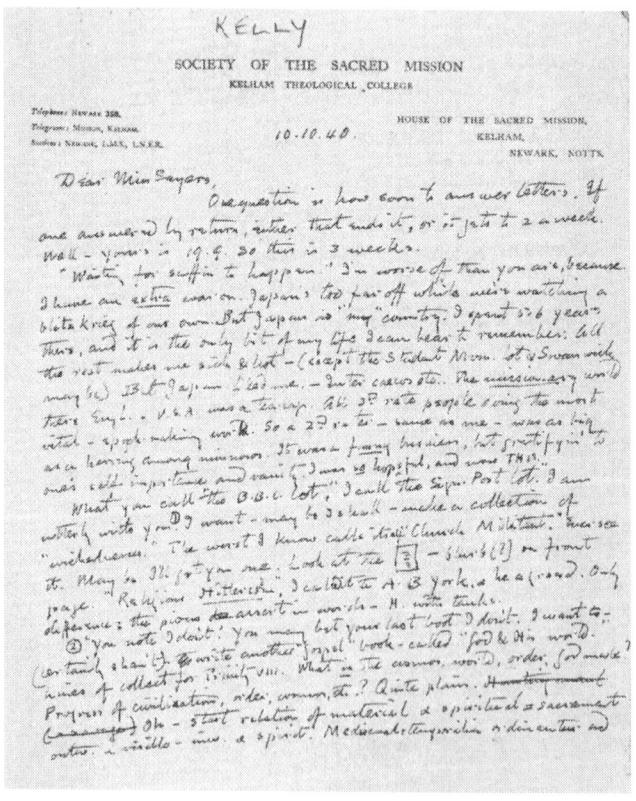

Herbert Kelly to Dorothy L Sayers, 10 October 1940

These boys (the students' Debating Society) played the Oxford Union. The motion was: 'A year of war in England – civil liberty has become nominal'. I told some of 'em – Austria, Bohemia, Poland, Romania, Denmark, Norway and France have all gone down talking of civil liberties – helpless before those who said: 'Everything for Germany'. Howsoever, we ain't Oxford. The motion was turned down 25 to 2 and a visitor.

Your *Mind of the Maker* sounds thrilling. Sounds rather like my dream of 'God and His World'. Do you know, I have a great idea that what folks are missing is any doctrine of the Holy Spirit. Aquinas's *Summa* says nothing of this. Loyola's 'Spiritual Exercises' misses it out blatantly. All Roman Catholics do and so do we. They – we – will talk *ad lib* about God and Christ – what He would like or what he would do; but never of God as operative. They get as far as 'God said' – and then they stop.[4]

> Yours sincerely in Christ
> Herbert Kelly S.S.M

PS. Re. 'Tec books – I'm a Victorian – on the side of the angels – and it's the only moral melodrama left. Ergo I could not read a *Raffles* book if you paid me 5 bob (not at the present price of cigarettes) I might *try* if you offered £200.[5]

---

[1] See note 4 to Letter 3.

[2] The subject was clearly on HK's mind at this time. A manifesto for the Order of the Church Militant is amongst his papers for 1940 (SSM/HK/MISC/12). The Order condemned such 'travesties' of Catholicism as papalism, 'with its Protestant individualism' and 'false piety' and waged a propaganda campaign to set up the Kingdom of God on earth.

[3] Collect for Eighth Sunday after Trinity, *Book of Common Prayer*, 'O God, whose never-failing providence ordereth all things both in heaven and earth; We humbly beseech thee to put away from us all hurtful things, and to give us those things which be profitable for us; through Jesus Christ our Lord. Amen'.

[4] This is a repeated theme of HK's teaching. He attacks what he sees as verging on the heresy of Christomonism in the church, where a Christocentric theology was preached to the virtual exclusion of the Holy Spirt. In his lecture notes on the Trinity, the book on the Holy Spirit is twice as thick as the other two volumes.

[5] See Introduction to this volume. HK discoursed in several articles on the value of detective fiction and irrelevance of the *Raffles* stories. *SSMQ*, Christmas, 1935.

Letter 37   House of the Sacred Mission
HK to DLS   Kelham

14 April 1941

Dear Miss Sayers

I got your book – I was honoured (really) and touched – but a little puzzled.[1] You do (I think) want to know my opinions of it?

Without express invitation (a) I am old (81 soon) and very slow. Further (b) I said a lot once before re. *The Zeal of.* Now reading this you know an awful lot – far more of St Augustine than I do. I see that in that letter I made a fool of myself!

As to the result I think it is rather wonderful. The main thing is that to me it is helpful – all kinds of perplexities are dealt with, and I can and will send boys to it. As the journalist said: 'The good paragraph is the liftable paragraph'. There is quite a lot I should like to lift into my lectures: bits stand out: 1. Creation, 2. The problem of nothing (which puzzled S. Anselm mightily). 3. Evil, 4. The chapter on 'Scalene Trinities', 5. The chapter on Problems (the best of all).

So far, I am thinking philosophically – in terms of my lectures. But I am applying it to myself and here I have a grievance. You write professionally, as a writer. Now, I have had my ambitions. Once I fancied myself as a preacher. Presently, about 1898 (or so) it became evident to me that no-one else did – so I just gave it up. I did think I might write something. Eventually, I laid two eggs – hatched 'em out – but they could have been better. A Gospel book[2] [and another] called *Catholicity*.[3] They never took on. I badly want to know why. I do have an idea: All the common perplexities of life have been stated by philosophers and scientists. I had studied them for over 40 years. I was/am convinced that the Creeds have an answer: which I tried to put quite simply for common (Swanwick) students (studying the arts, medicine etc.)[4] A very few brainy people (for example, the Archbishop of York) liked it [*Catholicity*] hugely.[5] Most professed they could not make out even what it was at, but I begged them in vain to show me the inconsistencies.

I guess you did not see anything in it – or you would have said so. I know nothing of the art of writing. Criticism seems to me mostly adjectives as I read it. Yours is the only piece I could follow.[6] If you have forgotten the book don't bother. It is too late now. I think my hope of writing anything effective has gone the way of my preaching – forty-three years ago. But if you could tell me whether it did seem to you poor, and why, I should like to know – don't be afraid of hurting. It is all past now.

Thinking of myself – according to your diagnosis – my one real creative activity was this College and Society. As a very ineffective curate, without scholarships or real brain power, I conceived an Idea. I wrote a book called *An Idea in the Working* (c. 1905), but the idea was consciously completed by the 1880s.[7] We actually started in 1890–91.

There were three ideas – 1) the fashion of a College; 2) of the Society (which was written in the Constitution of 1895); and 3) of the Education. The form given to them has never changed.

What was lacking was the Power to do things. The ineffectiveness of the curate was still there, till they turned me out in 1910. Now they have superiors – all Power but without Idea. The three forms go on (what you call 'ghost-ridden') but kept (more-or-less) on the Idea and its Incarnation which are inherited.[8]

I offer you this as an illustration of your principles in an institution where, unlike a book, there is a whole succession of 'fathers' each with his own notion of the original Idea. (For example, St Francis, who died protesting passionately against the Franciscan Order as it was shaping itself).[9]

Do I bore you? I am coming to a real point. After 1910 I was left to go on educating. I reverted to my old dream of writing. I was told to lecture on Church History and Dogmatics. I had an 'Idea' of History[10] (see the Collect for Trinity VIII as the great drama of God's purposes).[11] I wrote and re-wrote that course six or eight times – over forty years – as God gave me to see more.

Then they took me off that. Dogmatics is much more laborious. I got this history done – up to 1550 with the rest sketched in for the next man. I got the Psychology and Philosophy fairly good. The Dogmatics I shall never really get done.[12]

Now I am coming to business. First, we duplicate lectures. So that you can revise, re-write – as you will – every five or six years. Once more I had dreams of publishing a book. Quite a lot of good people found the history entrancing, but I do not think it will ever be published.

Second, this is the main point, writing books (fame) was a dream. God has taken away all, except this: teaching these boys. I was trying to teach them not to learn up History, but to understand men's minds – what God was doing – what they thought they were doing and what they missed. And not to learn correct doctrine with appropriate arguments, but to think them and see in them a Gospel to life, to science and to thought.

The Idea was to me quite clear – fifty years ago. Its Incarnation, in the method of teaching and in the lectures was reasonably good (anyhow in the History was). The Power, well about the results, I am utterly at sea. This side is always my weakness. I am never effective – not as a teacher or otherwise.

Are the boys any more intelligent than the ordinary clergy or graduate? Honestly, I do not know. Wish I did.

Now I come to what, I think, is the biggest problem/question in life. Can you help? The question of the ninety per cent. Take folk how you will – at school, college, etc. – ten per cent are really fond of games, of study, of art, music etc. and it is just about so with religion. Maybe ten per cent are contemptuous – 'anti' – while eighty per cent have some vague use for such things. Of the ten per cent, maybe ten per cent are really good.

My business is education. The University dons are the one per cent. I complain that they think exclusively of the ten per cent of clever chaps. They do not understand or care for the other ninety per cent. I do not say they are wrong. Maybe that is university business, but it is not the theological college business. 13,000 parsons – more or less by census – come from the ten per cent religious but they are not, cannot be, more than average intellectually. The dons can no more make them into scholars (even fifth rate ones) than the parsons can make the man-in-the-street 'religious' as they (don or parson) understand it in their different spheres.

I know that because I never could have been a scholar. Was it possible to get these ordinary folk to understand what thinking and knowing meant; and thence to see what God, a Gospel of God, meant in ordinary life, e.g. to shopkeepers, what it had meant always in history: that the ninety per cent, the religiously 'poor', to whom the Gospel is preached might have a faith to live by? That was the aim (Idea) of my Gospel book.

I put it as a question. Is it possible? Do they want to understand? Primarily, NO. The ordinary parson or soldier, farmer or (perhaps) doctor knows the routine way and rather resents having to think out a new method. Can they? I do not know; I am amazed how little they can get an idea – still less follow it up.

When I wrote to you first (re. *The Zeal* etc.) I had no idea how far you had thought, and I do not want to make the same mistake but, you have helped me so much. Here [in *Mind of the Maker*] you seem to me a bit caught yourself. I have two points:

Firstly, 'Creative art' – good, very good, but in the last chapter you join Middleton Murry and the rest (including our Father Hebert)[13] in reviling industrialisation etc. We do send you our *SSM Magazine*. In the last number I challenged that.[14] (If you do not get it or haven't looked at it tip me a p.c. and I'll send another). I want to know what you think of it. To my view the creative artists are an aristocracy (ten per cent), you have the point, quoting A.D. Lindsay: 'Saints are artists, ordinary people are not' and you add 'except in their personal (or family) life', and that is very helpful.[15]

But it does not seem to me in accord with what you say a few pages later where the economics do not seem to me in accord with the 'laws of the measurable' (i.e. material) nor the psychology with the common mind.[16] I do not think it hates its machine; it finds it a bit boring and disciplinary, like teaching stupid boys in a school. Someone has to do it. Ought they to hate it? As intensely creative, I am mainly conscious: 1) of a yearning to make a splash, 2) that in view of my ideals, I must want to do so – as the soldier craves victory; and 3) that I am a fool. I do not, thereby, envy the industrial worker. I, ego, me, am after all alongside Hitler and that's insanity.[17] The industrial worker is a bit of an animal. But he is a good sort. Middleton Murry seems to me to be grousing at common folk as God makes them.[18]

Please forgive me, are you sure you aren't too? In the Preface you write: 'worse than the dark ages'.[19] Oh Come! I can illustrate every point from the Middle Ages at their best. Ever read Duchesne, *Liber Pontificalis* (finest 'detective' fiction I know)?[20] I can send you a short summary of its achievements. Their capacity for inventing history and swallowing it were simply incredible. Try Armitage Robinson – 'Legends of Glastonbury'.[21] Reporters with a 'good story' are the heirs of monastic chroniclers with an 'edifying story' e.g. hagiography.

There are two differences:

1) the illiteracy you describe was then equally true of the best minds – e.g. Bonaventure's 'Life' of St Francis (see Sabatier).[22] Now it is a snare for the semi-educated who then did not count at all.

2) We do know better. You can say this and other people can. In the Middle Ages it never seems to have occurred to people that there was such a thing as lying: see the history of the Immaculate Conception and of Transubstantiation, later of the 'Assumption'. St Bernard rejected the first but followed the third (almost started it). Aquinas writhed under the second; but dare not challenge it nor look at its history.

Do let me say this. You have far more influence than I have, and more years to go. Don't – please don't – let Middleton Murry & co. (there's a lot of them) draw you into impatience with God's world as it is, and God's very stupid folk – I say it with tears – tears of patience. I believe quite solemnly that it is my own impatience with the stupidity of these, very average, children which has wrecked my 'power' (affective usefulness) as a teacher. But, in repentance; in confession and in amendment of life, I am going to try. Conversion at eighty-one requires a Miracle. But Aquinas says all conversions are miracles.

I have written a savage lot about myself. Still, it is your book mirrored in my life – as I see it.

I did want to make some notes on other points, but I have written too much as it is. It has taken me five days. I did think of getting it typed, but it is not worth it.

> Yours very sincerely in Christ
> Herbert Kelly SSM

[1] The book is *The Mind of the Maker*. This is, arguably, Sayers' most popular theology book. The chapters on 'Idea, Energy and Power', and 'The Energy Revealed in creation' are a development of much that she and HK discussed in earlier correspondence.

[2] Kelly, *The Gospel of God*, 1928.

[3] Kelly, *Catholicity*, 1932.

[4] I.e. not theologians.

[5] The Archbishop of York, William Temple, was a great admirer of HK's work. He wrote the foreword to the first edition. Their correspondence concerning *Gospel of God* is in the SSM archives (SSM/HK/SP/25/7).

[6] Presumably he sent a copy of *Catholicity* to DLS. Her comments have not survived.

[7] Herbert Kelly, *An Idea in the Working* (Kelham, SSM, 1908).

[8] In the chapter 'Scalene Trinities', DLS discusses writers who are 'ridden' by one or other person of the Trinity, and writes: 'all writers [...] tend to have their trinities permanently a little out of true', they are either 'father-centred', 'son-centred' or 'ghost-centred'. *Mind of the Maker*, pp. 125.

[9] Here HK speaks of his profound experience of alienation from SSM after he stood down as director in 1910. Internal politics, based around procedure and observance, broke out and the institution of SSM became barely recognisable to him. This period was later referred to as 'the Carleton Affair', and has been discussed by various commentators, see: Alistair Mason, *SSM: History of the Society of the Sacred Mission* (Norwich: Canterbury Press, 1993), pp. 125–134, Dewey, 'SSM Chronicle', pp. 107–118; and Alan Jones, 'Herbert Hamilton Kelly, SSM, 1860-1950: A Study in Failure', pp. 229–260, unpublished PhD thesis, 1971, Nottingham University.

[10] Little remains of HK's thoughts on this subject. A slip of paper with some scrawled notes in a copy of *Ad Fratres* (SSM/HK/SSM/19), entitled 'Idea of History' gives some idea.

[11] See note 4 to Letter 36.

[12] HK's lecture schemes are all available at the Borthwick Institute (SSM/HK/LS). The Dogmatics course ('doggies' as it was known to the students), went through many revisions and recensions (SSM/HK/LS/D).

[13] Arthur Gabriel Hebert, 1886–1963, Rector of Studies at SSM and prolific author.

[14] *SSMQ* Easter 1941, article by HK 'Industrialism and the Individual, pp. 2–7. Here HK sets out his theology of work.

[15] Kelly paraphrases the points discussed. The actual text by Sayers quotes A. D. Lindsay: 'The difference between ordinary people and saints is not that saints fulfil the plain duties which ordinary men neglect. The things saints do have not usually occurred to ordinary people at all [...] "Gracious" conduct is somehow like the work of an artist'. To which comment Sayers adds: 'The distinction between the artist and the man who is not an artist thus lies in the fact that the artist is living in the "way of grace", so far as his vocation is concerned. He is not necessarily an artist in handling his personal life [...]'. Sayers, *The Mind of the Maker*, pp. 155–6.

[16] Sayers, *The Mind of the Maker*, pp. 177–8.

[17] It is not clear what HK means by this unless he is referring to the common humanity of all peoples.

[18] This is an interesting comment on *The Mind of the Maker*. DLS has been accused of snobbery, especially in her novels. See *inter alia* Philip S. Scowcroft, '"Ludicrously Snobbish": How true is this of Sayers' detective fiction?', *Sidelights on Sayers*, 28, 1989, pp. 14–19. Certainly, the charge of intellectual snobbery is not altogether unmerited in *Mind of the Maker*. Kelly cites her Preface where she claims 'The education that we have so far succeeded in giving to the bulk of our citizens has produced a generation of mental slatterns' and proceeds that, particularly in the matter of Christian doctrine, 'a great part of the nation subsists in an ignorance more barbarous than that of the dark ages'. HK here appears to object more to the slur on medieval civilisation rather than on contemporary education. See Sayers, *The Mind of the Maker*, pp. xiv–xvi and 177–84.

[19] Sayers writes of the ignorance of the vast majority of the population in the matter of Christian doctrine which she sees as being due to 'a slatternly habit of illiterate reading'. Ibid p. xv.

[20] Louis Duchesne, *Liber Pontificalis* in two volumes, first published between 1886–1892. He could have included his own pamphlet: *Social Teaching of the Medieval Church*, 1925, here.

[21] Robinson J Armitage, *Two Glastonbury Legends* (Cambridge: Cambridge University Press, 1926).

[22] Paul Sabatier, *Vie de S. Francois D'Assis*, (Paris, 1900). HK developed a lecture series on St Francis, in which he compares the works of key biographers including Sabatier. He identified with St Francis as a 'failure' writing: 'Just at this climax stands St Francis, crying his warning: the righteousness of God is not won by dominion and power; it is love, joy, peace, and the road to it is by humility and meekness. But they would not hear' (SSM/HK/LS/C/10/12).

Letter 38   24, Newland Street
DLS to HK   Witham
                                                                   Essex

7th May 1941

Dear Father Kelly,

I wanted to answer your long letter at once, but I have been
trailing round the country, addressing H.M. Forces and various
civilian bodies about God, and Work, and Detective Fiction, to
the utter neglect and confusion of my proper job.

I'm very grateful you have found something worthwhile in *The
Mind of The Maker*. I sent you the advance proof because I couldn't
be sure when the thing was likely to actually get published, but I
didn't ask for advice and criticism as I had originally meant to do,
because I was so late in delivering the M.S. to the publishers that
I knew they jolly well wouldn't wait for reconstructions and altera-
tions. Distribution and marketing have got so slow and difficult
that they seem to want to go ahead with the printing and then have
a longish interval before publication. My first idea was that I
should get the book written quickly and collect all sorts of helpful
opinions so as to revise at leisure but, in the end, I was left struggling with the last chapter while the publishers uttered little refined
screams (Methuen's is a very gentlemanly firm) of impatience and
growing despair. So now it is in the press; but I still don't know
the publication date.

You mustn't think I really 'know an awful lot'. I don't – except
perhaps that I know something about the technique of my own
job. Since I started on this 'religious business' I've had to read a
little theology – far more than I ever dreamed of coping with
before – but I can't really call myself well grounded. Nor do I
know my St Augustine at all thoroughly – only of course one
couldn't write about the Trinity without seeing what he had to say.
As usual, I discovered that he meanly anticipated all my best

points. He's rather like Shakespeare in that respect – taking advantage of having been born a few centuries before other people to say everything that is to be said and saying it better. However, since the ordinary bloke doesn't read St. Augustine, it's probably quite a good thing to bring him out and offer him for inspection. Gosh! What a person that man was! But my theology is all bits and pieces. I suppose one ought to tackle it really properly – which involves coping with Aquinas, who depresses me, because he has a mind like a filing-cabinet, with everything ticketed away – 'Objection 1', 'Objection 2', with the appropriate rejoinders, till one wants to say 'Hi! My chief objection is to this unnatural neatness and symmetry – it's like being inside an enormous machine and I want to get out!'

As regards your own question: I think you have really answered it yourself haven't you? You say, 'I know nothing about the art of writing'. But it is an art with autonomous technique which executes itself in judgment on people who don't study it. It's like your illustration about the carpenter and the grindstone – he can get a better edge on in a few moments, without apparent exertion, than an amateur with any amount of time and sweat, but this is because he has learnt the technique through a lifetime of application. (There are apparent exceptions, like Bunyan – but then Bunyan had spent years and years reading the Bible, which is in itself a study of the best sort of technique for the kind of English he wanted to write). Actually, I think I should say that though the style of your writing is easy and familiar, taken sentence by sentence in detail, the presentation of your argument is obscure to the common reader because it leaps very swiftly from point to point without always distinctly showing the connection of ideas. It's rather like the modern kind of music, which passes directly from one unresolved discord to another, leaving the audience to supply the resolution in his head – which is what makes it so baffling to musically ignorant people like me. That is a quite legitimate technique for a specialist book addressed to the advanced and instructed reader, though not for a popular book; but each sentence considered by itself is addressed to a popular audience – so that what one gets is a kind of dislocation between the style of the whole and the style of the parts. You say that: 'a very few brainy people' found no difficulty with it: that was because they had the necessary knowledge of the subject as a whole to enable them to make the intermediate resolutions. But the average man is rather stupid and very ignorant, and needs to have all the 'bridges' built for him. (Much the same sort of thing is the trouble with my play *The Devil To Pay*, where the language is pretty simple but the intermediate resolutions much more complicated – at least, I judge that they must be so, since no critic has ever succeeded in making them, and your Brother George Every has damned the thing in a cheerful sentence which clearly betrays that he hasn't understood a single word of it. But then Brother Every thinks me a public menace and spends much effort in warning people off me.[1] God knows what he will say to *The Mind of The Maker*! A lot of 'criticism' is 'mostly adjectives', some of it very bogus; a lot more is chiefly concerned with technique, which is as dull and meaningless to those who don't care about technique as other people's 'shop' frequently is. I expect you like my book because it attempts to go to the principle behind the technique.

Your application of the trinity-analogy to the institutional sphere is very interesting and makes me hope that it is a true analogy for what it is worth. I fancy it is probably true also in the sphere of personality but haven't the psychological technique to pursue it along those dim and difficult paths.

Lastly, about ninety per cent and the 'machine age'. How frightful to be coupled with Middleton Murry, whom I find a most perverse and tiresome person! I don't want to abolish machines or anything of that kind. People whom I have consulted seem to disagree a good deal about whether workers find machine-minding a) a torture b) merely dull c) agreeable, I have heard tales of men in the Ford works who have gone mad and thrown themselves into the machines; in other cases, the workers just do the job without caring for anything except the money it brings them; finally, the highly-skilled men, running machines which make a real demand upon their intelligence, take the same pride and pleasure in them as the craftsman does in using his simpler tools. In addition, there seems to be some people to whom the performance of a monotonous job gives a real pleasure just because it is the one thing they can do perfectly, and so enjoy what Rudolf Adlers [sic] calls 'pleasure in right function'.[2] These last are all right; they have the proper delight in their work (I mean 'proper' in its exact sense – appropriate to its nature and theirs). And the skilled men are all right, *so long as economic corruption allows them to function as they should*; the trouble here, I gather, is that the need for filling the markets with cheap goods hastily made often debars them from using machines as good as they should be and from turning out work satisfactory to themselves. (I am told that these men will often walk out, if called upon to scamp the finish of their work – in wartime they can afford to, since their skill is at a premium; but in times when unemployment is acute, they cannot and must suffer the degradation of their 'creativeness'). The first class of men (the ones who go mad) may be the victims of brutal factory organisation, or they be plainly and simply in the wrong job, from which they ought to be extricated and set to do other things – and would be, if men cared more for the right use of men and machines than for commercial profits. The second class (the bored ones) ought, I think, to be catered for 1) by encouraging the creative use of their leisure – this is a second best but it is very useful; 2) by helping them to 'look to the end of the work', so as to ensure them what they are doing fulfilling a genuine human need – always supposing that the work on which they are employed *is* useful. These workers are, I fancy, in the majority, and, though perhaps not very brilliant people, could be helped to a much more active interest in their work and life if the society they serve were sufficiently enlightened and thought it worthwhile.

I have the *SSM Magazine*, but it has temporarily got swallowed up under a flood of pamphlets; so I'm not sure whether I've really tackled your point about industry. Middleton Murry and Co. have, I think, fallen into the usual error of externalising human sin and error and making it into a sort of irresponsible demon called 'Industrialism' (just as Hitler puts the blame for everything on Jews, and dissatisfied workers on the 'Capitalist Class'). It is true, I think, that machine-power and credit finance have put an extraordinarily efficient weapon in the hands of greedy men, and that we have failed to cope with it, largely because of a failure in imagination. But the great Demon that everybody is worshipping today is Economics, and it seems to be taken for granted that every prayer must be wound up, 'through Economics our Lord'. I don't believe you can cast out devils by Beelzebub; I think you've got to invoke a totally different power. But the whole question is immensely complicated; I am trying to get a book written about it by a man who knows industry from the inside.

'Illiteracy' – I am 'heated' about this. It is 'worse than the Dark Ages' because, so far as I know, people in the Dark Ages didn't exalt ignorance and stupidity into a virtue. Stupid, ignorant and credulous no doubt they were, but was the common man encouraged to go about crying, 'Thank God I have no brains!' as he is today? After all, the Dark Ages were *dark* – the common man hadn't much opportunity to check up on the facts offered for his assent. Today we build museums and libraries all round him, and then tell him that the people who make the arts and write the books are a set of degenerate highbrows, whose art and learning have no bearing upon experience. Our illiteracy is more barbarous than that of the Dark Ages simply because it is deliberate. I am not angry with stupid folk who are so by nature; but am desperately so with those who make a cult out of stupidity and with those extremely wicked people who exhort them to be stupid in order that they may exploit their ignorance, and who work upon them to hate and resent reason and beauty and imagination. 'We have driven the living imagination out of the world' said Yeats. I don't think artists are aristocracy, except in the sense that they are specialists in something which is common to every man, any more than saints, though an aristocracy, are the exclusive possessors of religion and virtue. Somebody (who?) defines sainthood as 'any one virtue wrought in heroic pitch'; we can't all bring our virtues or our creative artistry to the heroic pitch, but everybody ought to be able to enjoy active creativeness at whatever intensity is proper to him.

I apologise for the length of this letter, which seems to have got rather defensive and irritable. It comes from having done months of addressing people and arguing – whereas my proper job is making things with my imagination. What is especially tiresome is that there is a job I want to get down to – twelve radio plays for Children's Hour on the Life of Christ – which will be fun, only I foresee all sorts of fearful rows about it.[3] I've just got a line on Judas – which was holding me up a bit – only I don't know how I am going to make it intelligible to children, because it's rather subtle. The thing the Evangelists never trouble to explain is how anybody who was potentially good enough to be called as a disciple should also have been a wrong 'un from the beginning. He just comes on in the middle of the story, all set for villainy; but one can't suppose he is deliberately picked out because of his badness and put into the position where he could do himself and everyone else most harm. That would give a highly unpleasant flavour to the petition 'Lead us not into temptation' – and would be exactly the sort of thing one would expect from that hairy old wretch of a Jehovah who haunted one's childhood and was always looking for occasions to trip people up and 'come down sharp' on them. Oh, dear! And how little one knows, for dramatic purposes, of any of the Gospel characters! The domestic life of St Peter, for instance – he had a mother-in-law, how about his wife? What did she think of it all? The mother-in-law was healed. Was Peter glad to see the old lady restored, and does this indicate a happy domestic atmosphere? Or did he merely do the right thing by his wife, and regret the result? (This would make a pretty satiric comedy, though not for the Children's Hour!). Why are so many of the disciples just names, with no characters attached to them?

Maddening from the dramatist's point of view. What a pity that Our Lady has so little to say after the first scene or so. And (from the point of view of the Children's Hour) how hampering that all Christ's female acquaintances should have been so disreputable, except poor Martha, and, presumably, the women who turned up at the sepulchre. Salome the Mother of Zebedee's children has a little character, for she asked a foolish maternal question: I can see her – a good, pushful, anxious mother wanting her boys to get on in life; but how about the mysterious Joanna, wife of Chuza, Herod's steward? It's so interesting that the wife of Herod's steward should have been a follower of Christ, but *nothing* is told about her, or about what Herod's steward had to say to it all. Oh, well – the creative imagination thrives on difficulties.

    With very many thanks and all good wishes,

        Yours very sincerely,

          Dorothy L. Sayers

---

[1] George Every, 1909-2003, left SSM in 1973 and was received into the Roman Catholic Church. He taught at Oscott College, Birmingham, until his death. This refers to his book *Christian Discrimination* (Christian News-Letter Books series, Sheldon Press, 1940). He writes of DLS: '[…] the worst enemy of genuine Christian discrimination and genuine culture is not the philistine nowadays; it is the spurious cultural influence of well-informed young men and women on the arts side of some secondary schools and universities, whose idea of culture is a good display of literary references from the sixteenth and seventeenth centuries […] Those are the people who […] have given too ardently enthusiastic a reception to the new seriousness of Miss Dorothy Sayers. For a Christian fiction and a Christian drama must be very different indeed from the fiction and drama of the Boots Library public or of the Bloomsbury public, not only in their moral, in the solution of the problem in the last chapter, which Miss Sayers can always manage most ingeniously, but in their total moral effect. There the *Devil to Pay* was not so happy. Faust and Mephistopheles let rip with tremendous gusto, and then Faustus caught the last bus home. It would be a mistake to imagine that Christians ought to prefer every novel and play written by an intelligent Christian to every novel or play written by an intelligent sceptic', p. 62. (SSM/PP/60, part 1). DLS provides a vigorous response to this in her letter to Every of 25 June 1941 (Reynolds, *Letters, Vol II*, pp. 267-70).

[2] Probably Rudolf Allers, 1883–1963, Viennese psychiatrist and philosopher.

[3] She was right, *The Man Born to be King*, broadcast between December 1941 and October 1942, created much controversy. The BBC was accused of blasphemy for the portrayal of Christ by an actor who spoke in colloquial language. See Letter 41 below. Although it was attacked by both conservative Christians and by atheists, it also won critical acclaim.

Letter 39   House of the Sacred Mission
HK to DLS   Kelham

11 May 1941

My dear Miss Sayers

Thank you very much. Two main points.

1) Re my 'art of writing': it is very mysterious. You refer to this carpenter after a life of application. 'A bit hard'. I have done *nothing* but write for over fifty years, and with infinite pains. Everything – nearly – is written three or four times. And in result a very few (e.g. York) like it. Otherwise, all intellectuals e.g. my Prior, some in the house said exactly what you say. There are some funny things all the same. Several quite simple people found no difficulty (e.g. a girl clerk who did the typing).

2) The typescript was vetted very thoroughly at SSM but they made no objections. I tried in vain to get the Prior just to jot in the margins where the disconnections appear. Well, if you say so, I suppose it is. I suspect one difficulty has been all through my life I have always been trying to get a quart into a pint pot.

For myself, writing is a very common place practice. I have been struggling to equate everything – science, philosophy, history, observations of life so as a common place mind can see unity. As to style, I have always had to work on small canvasses, e.g. the Gospel Book. And those repeated writings were always efforts for terseness. If I had written all I wanted to say I might have done it in a 12/6 – I forced *masses* of stuff into a 2/6.

And my work here is to get real thinking into the heads of these dunces who do not even know what thinking is. I suppose you are right. I wish I had had folk to teach me – or to show me […] It is too late now. I must let it all go – like my beloved rock climbing. I am not the only person whose ambitions (hopes) were too big for the boots of his capacities.

Re. illiteracy etc. Very sorry. I quite agree.

a) There was a wonderful lot who made a cult of stupidity. To practical people it comes easy, e.g. farmers. Especially pious folk. I have heard a few. I think Pusey felt that way. Also, in the nineteenth century there were (I gather) a good few who thought preventative medicine – also the preservation of locusts – was interfering with 'providence'. A good many bitterly resent criticism of their own ideas (all party-minded folk, especially Church parties). Also, there have been 'wicked people' who objected to educating the 'lower classes' (J Austen, *Sense and Sensibility*).[1] Quite common in early nineteenth century and, I fear, in RC spheres (see the *Cambridge Modern History* – post Napoleonic Volume).

b) I should say much is open today. We do build schools and libraries because most of us don't feel thinking is a degeneracy, even if we are suspicious of people who can do what we can't. (e.g., write well). See St Bernard and Abelard, also the anti-rationalists. I have been having my ears boxed hard and am sore just now myself – so I don't like differing from anyone.

May I risk myself – as a priest – if I say don't be bitter over common folk? You've had a lot – 'addressing people and arguing' with very common and stupid people – who are frightened of you (e.g. the Baptists in *British Weekly*). Thank God, He lets you do it and that they will listen, they won't [to] me. It is awful hard to get people to see what they have never seen. After all, if God has made stupid people, we must be sympathetic over them – I take it He is.

However – let's let that pass. Sorry. Forgive me.

Further, re. Aquinas. I am rather fond of him. Filing is quite useful. What I do not like is the Blackfriars idea that you can get a whole real Christian faith into 2667 conclusions. Your book gives the real objection excellently in what you say about 'Problems'.[2] Absolutely.

Re. George Every. The difficulty with him is that he is badly bitten by the New Youth craze. It rather reminds me of:

Let the Christ rot
And the Hitler Youth
Go marching on.

I believe (have heard) that this verse is authentic. It hangs over the back of my mind like a dose of poison gas.

Re. Trinity. I did want to pass on a suggestion, very precious of me, from Genesis 1: 'and (i) God (ii) Said (logos) and (iii) so it was (by the Spirit)'. Noting that (ii) is in each case a single perfected purpose – final, and (iii) is a long process. Also, 'and (i) God (ii) spoke to (iii) Abraham', following all the Old Testament history until '(i) God (ii) spoke to God in the Son (iii) through the Spirit – on which all Christians follow.

One last – Bunyan learnt the art of writing from the Bible!!! I've read it a great deal, and I should have thought that – as you say – the sentences were all right; it is the 'connections' that are so difficult. I made my mind on Maurice and few men can follow his thinking.[3]

Please go on being patient with the old, tired, spent, disappointed, very jealous but still –

Yours sincerely in Christ
Herbert Kelly

P.S. I enclose another copy of *SSMQ*.

[1] It is not clear what the specific charge against Jane Austen is in *Sense and Sensibility*. She writes in the novel about education and reason versus emotional and Romantic responses, she also discusses the education of women (as accomplishments). Nowhere does she specifically mention the 'lower classes' in this context.

[2] I.e. chapter 11 'Problem Picture', in *Mind if the Maker*.

[3] Frederick Denison Maurice (see Introduction for his influence on HK).

Letter 40   24, Newland Street
DLS to HK   Witham
                                                       Essex

15 May 1941

Dear Father Kelly

I am so sorry if I seemed arrogant or rude. The whole thing is a mystery: and one person may toil all night and take nothing, while another gets more fish than he knows what to do with. Art is a jealous God that will be loved and served for his own sake and even then, he may have respect to one altar rather than another for no apparent reason. I only know that we must, apparently, be in love with the technique before it will do anything for one, 'kiss the son lest he be angry'.[1] (I've no idea *what* that really means, but it expresses what I mean!). From a purely practical point of view I'm sure you're right about the pint pot, violent confusion – packed writing – so as to cram a lot into the space, is always difficult reading, and the average reader hasn't the skill or patience to do his own unpacking. When I mentioned Bunyan, I wasn't then thinking about the sequence of ideas, but of the lovely lucid style which most people only attain after years of training through involved and elaborate writing, before they leave and discard everything but the essential. 'I saw a man clothed with rags, standing in a certain place, with his face from his own house, a book in his hand and a great burden on his back' and there's no doubt about the model of the style: 'He answered, Sir, I perceive by the book in thy hand that I am condemned to die and after that to come to judgment, and I find that I am not willing to do the first, not able to do the second'. 'Then the steward said within himself, what shall I do? For my lord taketh away from me the stewardship: I cannot dig, to beg I am ashamed, I am resolved what to do'. – It sounds so easy – every word like a living thing full of light and moving in its place like a dancer, but one has to love them before they will dance a step – love them I mean, not for what we can compel them to do but for what they are in themselves. But that seems to be a general rule – machines are just the same. I have an aunt who 'hates those wretched machines'; consequently they do everything to justify her dislike: cisterns refuse to work for her, door knobs come off in her hand, typewriters jam – one seems to have to know what the metal feels like inside if one is to handle it the way it likes.

(Sorry about these blots: a motorcycle exhaust went off like a gun just under the windows!)

Anyway I can't really explain it and am very sorry about sounding harsh and unsympathetic I didn't mean to be.

Thank you for sending the second copy of the *SSM Magazine*. I remember the article. I fancy that what the *Signposts* writers are trying – not perhaps very successfully – to say is that any appeal to identity, indeed any text of truth which contains the time factor – is doomed to fail under the judgment of time, where truth, like beauty, belongs to the 'mode of eternity'. They are, I expect, trying to cope with people like the correspondent who asked me: 'What is the up-to-date doctrine of the Trinity?', adding that he had not heard much about the Holy Ghost lately and wondered whether He was, so to speak, still doing business. One can't be surprised: one model of an aeroplane replaces another so quickly that people may be excused for imagining that new models of God are continually being issued. But as I tried to say in *Mind of the Maker* that line of thought contains a curious value of over-simplification. New forms of poetic beauty continually arise. But only add to the old without superseding them. But anything that commands respect merely because it is new and not because it is true is admitting in advance that it *must* be superseded, so that 'modernize' is (in that sense) outmoded in the moment of its birth. (On the other hand, a phrase whose truth time has distorted or made meaningless may become useless for establishing truth. 2+2=4 is a formula that time cannot corrupt, but when traditionalists insist on expressing this truth in phrases like that of the 'Dilly Song': 'Two and two are the lily-white babes a-clothed all in green-oh!' the common man may slightly object that this is ancient rigmarole that conveys nothing to his mind).

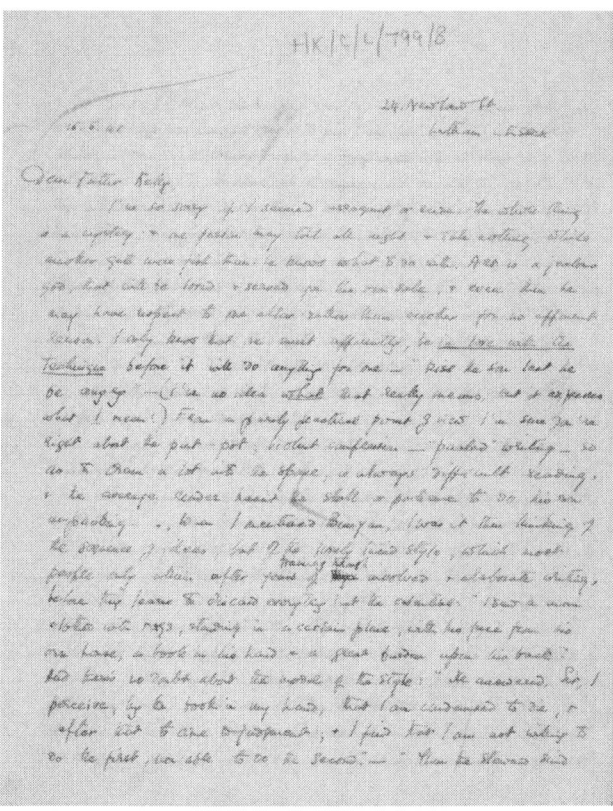

Dorothy L Sayers to Herbert Kelly, 15 May 1941

Oh dear, what is all this business about 'new youth'? It seems to be troubling people very much. Fr Widdrington is very concerned about it.[2] Your reference to Brother Every and the unpleasant anti-God anthems of the Hitler *Jugend* is alarming. I trust it is one of your sudden leaps of thought, that your Brother is not really preparing to march forward trampling the crucifix underfoot! Fr Widdrington's complaint, I gather, is that the 'Great Movements' are getting into the hands of the ungodly, that the bishops, poor blue-eyed innocents, are giving them their blessing without realising what it is about. But your suggestion of something sinister happening among the very elect is still more disquieting. My only criticism of Brother Every so far is that he is apt to generalise on insufficient knowledge, and that he is imbued with the idea that whatever is popular must be bad – two common errors of youth which time will amend. (He makes rather wild statements about architecture for instance, and I don't think he knows very much about Medieval mystery drama, and he is something of a literary snob as the young and doctrinaire tend to be – but which of us, remembering our own past, is entitled to cast stones about that sort of thing?)

Bitter? Well, I don't know, I like laying about me. I like seeing the tables of the money lenders go bumping down the steps of the Temple. But it's not my proper job, which is to show in story form and not to argue or exhort. So that I always have the irritating sensation that my time is being wasted, accompanied by a strong sensation of guilt for allowing it to happen. I'm not called to be a fisher of men. I don't handle the fish roughly unless they have come with the express intention of breaking the net. I had a despairing letter the other day from a man who said he couldn't believe anything – having apparently never been introduced to any ideas beyond, on the one hand, the hairy old horror of a Jehovah in a nightgown and, on the other, a humanist Jesus of the 'liberal school'. The poor fish couldn't make anything of this fantastic assortment, and I don't blame him. I suggested some books to read and said I thought he needn't worry too much about till somebody has shown him what he was expected to believe in. Also, that every science, including theology, had its technical terms, which really did stand for something and was worth finding out how they were used, because it would then be easier to make some sense of the argument. All this seemed a new idea to him, he has ordered the books and made a resolve not to be impatient with the parson! But *I* am impatient. Here is an intelligent, humble-minded, 'middle-class public-school man' of 35 – and it is an absolutely new idea to him that 'religious belief is founded upon a conviction that the universe is intended to, and does, make sense. What in the devil's name have we been doing to people like him? What would Aquinas have said if he knew that to this pathetic product of an enlightened civilisation, the concept of an ordered universe represented the believer and not the bridge between the 'Rector's Christianity' and 'mine' – to quote his own words. Let's have Aquinas back by all means, and even the 2667 conclusions, rather than the nightmare muddle out of which people have to be hauled by passing detective-novelists in a hurry and with no proper tackle! I've had to talk to 'H.M. Forces' too – any amount of interest there, plenty of intelligence – but it's hard to find language they understand; one can't make any progress, because one has to begin by defining all the time. Mrs Bell (Bishop of Chichester's wife) has an evacuee girl for a parlour maid and sent her to some kind of Sunday class. Girl returned delighted: it was so interesting – before she had always thought the Holy Spirit was something you put in a lamp and set light to. Sermons and services pour over people's heads because nobody will trouble to define terms or say what doctrine IS – no wonder the wretched fish are bewildered half the time, one only has to state the thing in intelligible terms and they say, 'Oh yes, we quite agree – but we thought it was something else'. All I ever do is to go about imploring people not to be so *silly* and to find out what a statement means before they either reject or swallow it wholesale. But I still say it isn't my job, and if God lets me do it, it must be in the dubious spirit of someone obliged to open a packing-case with a corkscrew in the absence of the proper implements. And in the end, I shall come out all the wrong shape and Our Lady will say, 'Dear me, Father Noah, what have they been doing with the corkscrews?' and Father Noah will say, 'Yes, indeed, mum, and the packing cases aren't good for nothin' but firewood either'. And all the cherubs will wipe their little eyes with their little wings and look at the racks and racks of bottles full of Unwritten Entertainment and Fine Old Crusted Mystery and wish for a corkscrew and make common cause in distress with the common man. I don't despise the common man and I don't frighten him. It was the stagehands and the callboys and the bar waitresses who used to nip round when they had a minute free to watch the angel scenes in *Zeal of Thy House*, and the common soldiers who said the 'Creation speech' was the best bit of the play. But there are a lot of half-educated two-timers playing hell-and-tommy with the common man, who won't either think themselves or let the common man think, and who've got to be smitten, even if it's only with the jawbone of this particular ass. Still, Balaam's ass feels it's a pity, having once had the chance to speak literally instead of scavenging about.[3]

Yes, that's a grand suggestion about 'God said… and there was' a whole long process of power. The common man could understand that, I think, but not if his mind is cluttered with nightgowned Jehovahs and humanist Jesuses preaching ethics and Holy Spirits that live in methylated spirit bottles.

This is a long, stupid, disconnected letter – don't be bothered with it. You are old and wise and have charity to spare for the 'blind moths'. But they've left the sheep in such an unhappy huddle, the poor things bleat under the window, and what is one to do with them, if one isn't a shepherd by nature? Leave what one's doing (cursing loudly), throw out a turnip or two and then block the shepherds' paths with their own crooks! I don't mean only the clergy – but also, and far more, the people who undid the door of the fold, led the sheep out into a 'larger liberty' and now have the neck to abandon them in a nasty wilderness, saying loudly that the Church should have looked after them better.

I think I've been a bit upset by the poor bloke who 'couldn't believe anything'. I was afraid I was being severe with him – urging him to stop crying and give his brains a chance. Instead he was pathetically grateful and thanked me for 'being gentle with him', and received the baldest statement of what Christian doctrine was supposed to be about as if it was a revelation from heaven. Why should anybody have been made so unhappy for lack of a plain statement? Why should the poor wretches be left so bedevilled and bewildered? Why should they be left to the mere chance of writing to a perfect stranger to get the smallest inkling of what the whole things is about?

Anyway, I must stop and try to 'unpack' the God-the-Son portions of the Creed in six ten-minute BBC talks! I have just realised that the whole document is one solid mass of technical terms none of which means anything to the ordinary man of today!

Yours, feeling very much the ass's jawbone.

D.L Sayers

No correspondence has survived for the years 1942 or 1943 but the context of later letters suggests there was an ongoing exchange during this period.

---

[1] From Psalm 2:12. The King James version has 'Kiss the son lest he be angry and you perish in the way', the Hebrew is rather different: 'Do homage in purity, lest He be angry and you perish in the way'. The NRSV has: 'Serve the Lord with fear, with trembling kiss his feet'.

[2] P.E.T Widdrington was founder of the quarterly magazine, *Christendom: A Journal of Christian Sociology*. Christian Sociology was primarily an Anglo Catholic Christian Socialist inspired intellectual movement with which DLS, T. S. Eliot and R. H. Tawney were connected. Fr Reginald Tribe SSM was another advocate and his 'small primer on Christian Sociology', *The Christian Social Tradition* was published in 1935. In the 1930s the movement took a particular stand on unemployment and the worth of work, promoted by Bishop William Temple among others. For a discussion of its development see David Lyon, 'The Idea of a Christian Sociology: Some Historical Precedents and Current Concerns', *Sociological Analysis*, Autumn, 1983, Vol. 44, pp. 227–42.

[3] Book of Numbers 22: 21–39.

Letter 41   24, Newland Street
DLS to HK   Witham
                                                             Essex

20 April 1944

Dear Father Kelly

I was so glad to get your letter.[1] I have been meaning for a
long time to write to you, but what with one thing and another it
didn't seem to get done. I keep on finding myself without a cook,
or without a secretary, or without either of them, and in trying to
do my own chores I get behindhand with everything.

I will deal briefly with Mr Krusseft when he comes along, but
I'm afraid I won't be able to get to Durham. For one thing long
journeys are rather difficult when I am so much tied at home[2], and,
for another, I have temporarily given up appearing on religious
platforms. The amateur theologian soon loses his first 'surprise
value' and becomes 'one of the old gang'. At first, it's a salutary
shock to people when a detective novelist bursts out with a
defence of dogma – but before long one is only 'old Sayers again,
of course, who's gone pious in middle age'. And while declining
into an ineffective speaker, one is apt to forget how to write! I've
only written one long or important thing since *The Mind of the
Maker*, that is the cycle of Radio plays on the Life of Our Lord:
The Man Born to be King. You may have heard of all the row there
was about it when it was first broadcast in 1942.[3] The Lord's Day
Observance Society and the Protestant Truth Society moved
heaven and earth to get it stopped. Spending a lot of money in ad-
vertisements, asking questions in the House, petitioning the King,
invoking on all our heads a variety of assorted curses out of the
Book of Revelation saying that God was so angry about it that He
had caused all sorts of disasters out of spite and offended dignity.
However, the BBC Religious Advisory Council dug their toes in,
all of them with one accord, from the Roman Catholics to the
Welsh Evangelicals and the Protestant gentlemen from Ulster –
and the House of Commons, and the BBC and the captains of

hundreds and the captains of thousands and all the rest of them were so staggered at hearing the Church speak with a united voice for the first time since the Reformation that they let the thing go through. I don't believe I ever sent you a copy of the book when it was published. As a matter of fact I sent out very few 'complementaries' [sic]; as the whole edition was practically sold out on publication and it didn't seem fair; but I'm sending one now in the hope that you will like it and find the theology reasonably sound. (It must, at least, be fairly 'central' for I have been mistaken for an R.C. and a Methodist on the strength of it!).

I shall look forward to seeing Bro. Every's book on the Eastern Church.[4] The other day I read Dr Zernov's little book *The Church of the Eastern Christians*,[5] which was so attractive that I almost want to rush out and get converted to Orthodoxy immediately. There seemed to be so many points on which the Eastern attitude to things corrected, or at least complemented, the Western, and had a warmth and richness and charity and imagination which is lacking in the legalism and formality of the West. Why have we been ignorant all this time about the Eastern Church? I shall be meeting Bro. Every on Thursday at a committee about Religious Broadcasts and will ask him more about it. We have met before: he violently disapproves of almost everything I write, and I disagree with most of what he says about architecture and Christian discrimination, but we have corresponded in a friendly way and always behave nicely when we meet in the flesh!

Like you I am more concerned about causes than personalities though I recollect, with some disquiet, that somebody once said that this attitude was the sin of Judas, or the way to the everlasting bonfire, or something. But it is always the craftsman's attitude: 'let me perish, but let my work go on'. I put that into Willian in *Zeal* and it's true, I think, for all craftsmen. We are made that way.

Thank you for all your kindness

Yours very sincerely

Dorothy L. Sayers

[1] This letter has been lost.

[2] Her husband, 'Mac' Fleming, was an invalid and becoming increasingly difficult and unpredictable at this time.

[3] See note 3 to Letter 38 above.

[4] Probably *The Byzantine Patriarchate 451-1204*, which was published in 1947.

[5] N. Zernov, *The Church of the Eastern Christians* (London: SPCK, 1946).

Letter 42   SSM
HK to DLS   Kelham

15 August 1946

My very dear Friend

(NB. I got out of bed specially to get a posh sheet to write to you on, and it has been absorbing dust for years).[1]

NB. 2 Why do the copybooks assert that 'circumstances alter causes'? I do not see that it is an especially good statement. Let us rather say 'circumstances affect the value of incidents'.

I got into correspondence with Gregory Dix OSB over confirmation and sent him (by permission) a short essay on Trinitarianism re the 'Work of the Spirit'.[2] There were only three or four typed pages which he called 'packed dynamite'). I cannot do anything (as you know), but he can. I wonder if you people who can realise how self-importance grinds at the people who CAN'T.

Well, I got into a dry patch and you, who have so much to say, remembered me and sent me your little book.[3] 'The dry patch' (aforementioned) considerably affected the value of the *sending*. So does the *matter* of the book. I have read it four times. Yes, that helps in the dry patches. I think the sum of it is the airman's last speech on p. 76. The sorrows, anxieties etc. of life mostly come down to self-importance. I am reading Miller: *The Xian Significance of Marx*.[4] Quite *ad rem*.

Yes, I do wish I could see and hear. Last month I turned my eighty-sixth lap. My beloved Manchester doctor was here yesterday. He and I came up to my room – forty stairs – at the top he threw his arms round me and laid his head on my breast (embarrassing?); then he said: 'strong as a horse' (disappointing?). He was listening to my heart! I knew the blighted thing was all right.

I do not like to ask you to write to me but if – when – should – you do so, could you let me know where your seven deadly virtues are?[5] Second thoughts, don't bother, I'll find 'em. We've got two pamphlets somewhere.

Yours affectionately in Christ

Herbert Kelly SSM

---

[1] There are almost certainly letters leading up to this which have been lost.

[2] Gregory Dix, 1901–1952, Anglican Benedictine monk at Nashdom Abbey, Buckinghamshire. Kelly sent Dix a typed paper 'The Holy Spirit and Confirmation' in the summer of 1946. The paper develops ideas touched on by Kelly here: namely life work, failure and God's purpose in all the mess of life. Kelly dwells on his own life and draws on patristic, theological and Scriptural references (with the Athanasian Creed, Augustine and the decadence of the Middle Ages thrown in for good measure) to try to understand 'the mess'. It is in the somewhat chaotic style of his letters to DLS but shows him still to be grappling with faith and understanding. Dix responded: 'You still have ideas, all right!' and commented 'I have rarely received so much dynamite in so neatly packed a parcel'. (SSM/HK/C/L/815/2). Dix and Kelly had corresponded a few years earlier on the creeds and catechesis and Dix wrote then 'Fr Herbert always catechizes me on things I know nothing about and have to look up', letter 29 December 1943 (SSM/HK/C/L/810).

[3] The book must be The Just Vengeance, a play written by DLS for Lichfield Cathedral and performed there in June 1946. One of the main characters is an airman and the theme of the play is atonement. I am grateful to Margaret Wiedmann of the Dorothy L. Sayers Society for identifying this work.

[4] Alexander Miller, *The Christian Significance of Marx* (London, SCM, 1946).

[5] In a short essay entitled *The Dogma is the Drama*, DLS identified the seven Christian 'virtues' as: 'respectability; childishness; mental timidity; dullness; sentimentality; censoriousness; and depression of spirits'. She went on: 'Whenever an average Christian is represented in a novel or a play, he is pretty sure to be shown practising one or all of the Seven Deadly Virtues enumerated above, and I am afraid that this is the impression made by the average Christian

upon the world at large'. It was published together with another piece, in *Strong Meat* (London: Hodder & Stoughton, 1939).

Letter 43   SSM
HK to DLS   Kelham

8 March 1947

My very dear friend

It was so nice to get your letter and your inscribed book.[1] It is a lot of help – more than you'd think – when you are nearing eighty-seven you are apt to get shut in. Not that I'm not sur-rounded with grinning boys rushing in to help me down the beastly stairs – or up them. Forgotten? No indeed – it was about the 'Seven Deadly Virtues' on p. 23. But I am most glad to have the book whole. You and I are fighting shoulder to shoulder: fifty or sixty years ago I was proclaiming 'Our C of E trouble is that the clergy have been taught orthodoxy and ruined their real aim which is to think. It is connected (a) with a Ritschlian cult of religion versus theology (feeling and conduct),[2] but also (b) with the RC definition of 'Faith' as the acceptance of statements (cf. 'Faith' in the *Catholic Encyclopaedia*).

We have got a new Warden for the Theological College: a boy of our own, and all studies are in his hands.[3] The Director is a POWER!! But I don't think he understands our theology a bit.[4]

I should have written earlier, but I have been making my way – deadly slow – through some jobs on 'order'. (1) for our *SSM Quarterly*, turning on Prof. James' priceless 'everything comes to us as fragments torn out of a whole'.[5] I expect you get it. If not, I'll see you do. I do take such pains and it is such slow work. I described my life once as spent trying to get a quart into a pint pot. Can you get theology, philosophy, sciences, history into a fourth class mind? But it is the same with these boys of ours. I am always trying to condense the Universe into four pages.

Just as your letter came, I got an order for a short review of *Vocation*, which he wants to palm off on the Bishop of Southwell. Now, from this I turn back to a message to Japan, my beloved country. I wonder if you know what happened? The Japanese government decreed that the church must be Japanese: no Bishops or money from abroad (HK: loud cheers), then next, 'all Christians must join in one church' (NB. Except the RCs – presumably because Italy was an ally), then all my boys – who included most of the Japanese bishops – dug their toes in, so there was trouble. Some bishops gave in (not mine) so there was a schism. That is healed and now there is opportunity calling to them. Please pray for them.

> Yours sincerely in Christ
> Herbert Kelly, SSM

We have been asked to take over Australia. Your fellow citizen, Fr Snell has gone out for the Theological College work.[6]

[1] This letter has been lost.

[2] HK is referring here to the teaching of Albrecht Ritschl, 1822–1889, who developed an ethical-social approach to theology.

[3] Theodore Smith, warden from 1945–1962. He left to become a Roman Catholic and died in 1965.

[4] The director was Stephen Bedale, 1888–1961.

[5] 'Wisdom-Knowledge-Faith' in *SSMQ*, Easter 1947. This is a complex piece that shows HK's thought process and reasoning still to be in good order. 'Prof. James' is William James, 1842–1910, American philosopher, historian and psychologist. The source of the quotation cannot be identified: HK gives no reference. James was an inspiration to Kelly at this time: he quotes from him in an earlier paper 'The Catholicism of Rome', *SSMQ* Christmas, 1932, and in *Catholicity*, p. 41.

[6] SSM opened a theological college in Australia in 1947. Stephen Bedale, Basil Oddie (the first Provincial) and Antony Snell facilitated the initial setting up (see Dewey, 'SSM Chronicle', pp. 214–5).

Letter 44   SSM
HK to DLS   Kelham

10 July 1947

My Dear Miss Sayers
     You must – I hope you do – count me as a humble admirer.
Is it a fall from grace if I sometimes criticise? It is rather late to go
back to your *Begin Here*[1] but I am very jealous of the Maritain cult
of the Middle Ages.[2] Do you read Coulton?[3]
     There is a passage in that book: 'The theological conception
up to the Reformation was of one sovereign, not of this world.
This consists of a) The individual through his lord to the king, to
the Church, and to God had free access to the rule of law b)) God
whose ruling was immediately ascertainable from the Church
authorities who were ordained to expound and explore it'.[4]
     As to a) I am a little doubtful. If I remember right a villein
could not sue his lord til' the fourteenth century. Secondly, in
theory one could appeal to Rome, but it was not at all 'free' it was
very expensive. See St Bernard (*De Consideratione*) only bad men
appealed, and they generally won their case because they brought
business (i.e. fees). Thirdly, in any case Pius II declared that an
appeal to a general council was heresy. Fourthly, there was certainly not appeal to 'God'. When Hus so apostatised (in
Constance) that was at once declared heresy. In fact, it is incon-
sistent with b). The recognised Church authority is the sole
speaker for God – *Vicarius Dei*.
     You say: 'it failed because the human instrument failed to
realise its implications'. I should say 'because as in b) it was bent
on realising them. Boniface VIII, *Unam Sanctum*: is altogether
necessary to salvation that every creature be subject to the Roman
pontiff'.
     In sum, the Medieval papacy is the first instance of a
totalitarian state (and the Inquisition the first Gestapo). It differed
from Germany and Italy because the bureaucracy secured the right

to appoint their own Commander-in-Chief. I fancy it did in Japan. There is a direct historical connexion. Figgis argues (and proves) that the absolute kingship – *De jure divino* – began by the monarch's claiming the same *plentitudo postestatis* (*intemporialibus*) as the Pope.[5] The Papacy has never gone back on it (see enclosed quotation from Pius X (1906).[6] What is this but dictatorship? And then, does GOD mean anything? Hitler and Stalin saw that two faiths could not co-exist. The *Duce* could not afford a quarrel on his own doorstep and compromised. The Pope? Well – from the 13th century: 'It was essential for the laity to carry out 'obligations' – rules (mass, confession and communion once a year) and for the rest it was sufficient to believe that there was a God who recompenses'. There was no hint of access. It was on this that the Protestant revolt turned, though, with the same craving for a 'material voice', it reverted to fundamentalism. The Pope had shut out God nearly as effectively as Stalin.

The principle is, I think, given in Khomiakoff [sic] – see card two[7] and re. the Holy Spirit, it is quite remarkable how little the RCs can make of it. Aquinas is poor, Loyola's spiritual exercises virtually confine it to the Hierarchical Church.

Please forgive. I am just so nearly cut off from doing anything now, that I feel a sort of craving to supply bits of ideas, such as I have, to people still alive in the world, who can use them.

Yours Sincerely in Christ

Herbert Kelly SSM

If you should feel interested in the Abbot of Burton, Loyola or Innocent IV – you probably know all about them, but, if you don't – it would be a joy to save you the trouble of looking them up.

---

[1] Sayers, *Begin Here: A Wartime essay* (London: Victor Gollancz, 1940).

[2] Jacques Maritain, 1882–1973, possibly a reference to his *Antimoderne* (1922) in which he gives a critique of modern thought.

[3] George Gordon Coulton, 1858–1947, historian, medievalist, and controversialist. He was anti-Catholic and anti-clerical. His books include *The Medieval Village (Medieval Village, Manor and Monastery)* (1925); *The Miracle of the Blessed Virgin Mary* (1928); *The Medieval Scene* (1930); *Ten Medieval Studies* (1930), any of which HK may have had in mind.

[4] In *Begin Here* Sayers traces a cultural history of human thought with political, social and economic consequences. She describes the vison of humanity as 'theological' in the period up to the Reformation with a concept of divine sovereignty which encompassed equality under God and the value of human nature, arts and crafts. The Reformation ushered in the 'humanist' period in which she identified man's understanding of his value as separate from God.

[5] John Neville Figgis, 1866–1919, historian, philosopher and member of the Community of the Resurrection (Mirfield) wrote, *inter alia*, *The Divine Right of Kings* (1896).

[6] HK attached various bibliographic notes to this letter. One is entitled 'RC re. Authority' quoting Pius X and taken from Daniel T. Jenkins, *Nature of Catholicity* (London: Faber & Faber, 1942).

[7] Alexei Khomyakov, 1804–60, Russian theologian and philosopher, his letter giving impressions of England was reproduced in W. J. Birkbeck, *Life and Letters* (1922). The second enclosure to this letter is a quotation from the same work and entitled 'Ascension'. 'Why was it expedient that Our Lord should *leave* his church, and why did the disciples *rejoice*? [Surely…] it was the Holy Spirit […] that the kingdom of God should dwell *within* men and the unity must exist as a result, not a cause, of the inward. We are united to the Church because we are members of the whole body and of Christ.' ('Ascension', p.135.)

Letter 45   24 Newland Street
DLS to HK   Witham
                                                             Essex

24 July 1947

Dear Father Kelly

    It was very good to hear from you again. I hope you are keep-
ing well – that you don't mind this thundery, and to me stupefying,
weather. I hear of you now and again from Brother George Every,
from whom I am at this moment seeking guidance in the matter

of Pope Anastasius II, confined so unkindly by Dante in a large red-hot tomb at the edge of the circle of the Heretics.

Oh dear me! *Begin Here* – that was a very rush job, undertaken much against my will and in a distracted state of mind, at the desire of my publisher, who wanted a 'wartime' message from me. Publishers think that no war is complete without a series of 'messages' from all kinds of people. Most of them, written, are only fit for pulping, and, with any luck, they get pulped and forgotten. The whole book teems with errors and omissions – and indeed I scarcely remember myself what is in it.

As regards the medieval theory of the hierarchies – I should be the first to admit that it was never properly put into practice. The implication of the theory is that obligations work downwards as well as upwards: and that is the point at which the practice always tended to come a cropper. (Whether in fact the villein was always as helpless as he might appear, I don't know. In this country, custom and the manor court, to say nothing of expediency, probably made the lord mindful, in some degree, of his duty to those below him). But there was a theory of hierarchy, just as today there is an egalitarian theory, which is equally belied by practice. One might say, I suppose that any political theory would work, if only people would work it. Still, there the theory was – magnificent in conception, deplorable in the carrying out: very far removed from its heavenly counterpart in the *Paradiso*, each sphere drawn by love to the one above it and drawing the one below it! (I used, of course, the more familiar Western theory, by which the spiritual power is set above the temporal, rather than the more complex *De Monarchia* theory of the two powers, chiefly because it was the less complex and more familiar; not because I personally prefer it). If I remember rightly, the point of the theory which I wanted to emphasise (since it is only theories that I was comparing) was that the structure embraced the totality of man, in his whole nature, and did not pick out a special aspect of him –

economic, rational or what-not – as the sole political unit which counted.

Yes, I know Coulton: he worries the vicar of the parish who hovers over me in fish queues demanding to know what he is to think of him! Like all historians with a strong bias, he is stimulating to read, though one does have to allow for the bias. It is extraordinary how people divide into two camps about the Middle Ages – often one wouldn't think they could be talking about the same period. Very often, of course, they are. The nineth century in Byzantium is not very like the nineth century in England, and both are very unlike the fourteenth century in Italy. In some ways I think the High Middle Ages would have suited me very well – I don't mind about sanitation, and I would just as soon have Guelf-Ghibelline riots as doodlebugs. But I always come up against the question of Tea. The thought of starting the day on swipes or sour wine is alarming to me.

This you, will rightly say, is a frivolous reply to a serious rebuke. But I admit all the weaknesses of *Begin Here*. Only the book is dead now, thank God! and will never be resuscitated. So, I can't feel very strongly about it. What I *do* feel, very strongly indeed, is the likeness between the Middle Ages and our own time, at almost every point *except* the unity of its theological assumptions. On all the bad sides, the two periods are horribly alike – the uncertain tenure of life, the violent political divisions (only now on a larger scale), the return in many places to a new kind of serfdom – but worse now because not attached to the land (the gap made now at a new level) between the unlettered and the lettered, the emergence of the new and the crushing forms of despotism. I should be glad to know that we are on the way out of the new Dark Ages, but I am rather afraid we may be just about to plunge into them. However, I dare say the first two or three centuries are the worst!

In the meantime, I get on with translating Dante. In the course of annotating him I shall have every opportunity to deal with the claims of the Papacy. I do not know how that man escaped being burnt alive. He was anything but a docile member of the flock, and was quite prepared to teach orthodoxy to the Vatican.

Pius X – *Vehementer* is marvellous.[1] But ever since Trent, Rome has been intellectually as dead as mutton. (Yes, I am aware that this is an exaggeration). One of the big troubles is that, whereas in the Middle Ages, your intelligent lay theologian would no doubt have meekly accepted the theory and then heavily trounced pope, bishops, clergy and every actual person concerned as a bunch of ignorant, corrupt, evil-living, venal, heretical and hireling shepherds, the modern RC feels bound to pretend that all actual RC ecclesiastics live up to the theory. It's astonishing what you could get away with in the fourteenth century, provided you struck to the doctrine and only flogged its official exponents. Nowadays you can say that Christ is a myth and the Church a fraud, and nobody cares two hoots: whereas if you say that Bishop X is a liar and the Dean of Y a blackmailer, you go to gaol. But in the Middle Ages it was the other way round – provided of course, you kept out of the way of the Bishop's men-at-arms and didn't happen to live in the Dean's cathedral close.

Yes, I do feel rather at home in the Middle Ages.

With many thanks – and if the opportunity presents itself I will try to be less sketchy about the hierarchical theory in the future.

> Yours ever
> [DLS]

---

[1] The papal encyclical *Vehementer Nos* promulgated by Pius X in 1906. In this he strong denounced the separation of Church and State in France following the repeal of the Concordant of 1801 between Napoleon and Pius VII.

Appendices

List of Letters

The letters contained in this volume represent the complete surviving correspondence between Herbert Kelly and Dorothy L. Sayers which has never been published in its entirety. The correspondence used is kept in the SSM archive collection at the Borthwick Institute, York University and is composed of original and copied letters.

Copies to complete the set were given by Sayers' son, Antony Fleming, to Margaret Dewey, librarian at SSM, Willen Priory, in 1982. The photocopies completed the SSM collection and in exchange Dewey sent copies of the SSM side of the correspondence. Fleming was compiling the letters and writings of his mother for publication. He died before he was able to complete this work, but it was taken on by Barbara Reynolds. The originals are now at the Marion C. Wade Center, Wheaton College, Illinois [MCW]. The MCW Folder numbers are given.

All the reference numbers given are SSM ones. The HK/C/L/799/ series are originals (or carbon copies) which have been kept in the SSM archives, the HK/C/L/[799A] range are copies from the MCW collection. The MCW references for the originals are also listed here.

Date	Letter Number	Ref	From	Original at
1/10/1937	1	HK/C/L/799/1	HK to DLS	SSM
4/10/1937	2	HK/C/L/799/2	DLS to HK	SSM
14/10/1937	3	HK/C/L/799/3	HK to DLS	SSM
20/10/1937	4	HK/C/L/799/4	DLS to HK	SSM
23/11/1937	5	HK/C/L/[799A]/1	HK to DLS	MCW/261
25/11/1937	6	HK/C/L/[799A]/2	DLS to HK	MCW/261
8/2/1938	7	HK/C/L/[799A]/3	RR to DLS	MCW/261
7/2/1938	8	HK/C/L/[799A]/4	DLS to HK	MCW/261
[February 1938]	9	HK/C/L/[799A]/5	HK to DLS	MCW/261
17/2/1938	10	HK/C/L/[799A]/6	DLS to HK	MCW/261
21/2/1938	11	HK/C/L/[799A]/7	DLS to HK	MCW/261
14/3/1938	12	HK/C/L/[799A]/9	HK to DLS	MCW/261
25/3/1938	13	HK/C/L/[799A]/10	HK to Mrs. Bear	MCW/261
25/3/1938	14	HK/C/L/[799A]/11	HK to DLS	MCW/261
[April 1938]	15	HK/C/L/[799A]/12	HK to DLS	MCW/261
Palm Sunday	16	HK/C/L/[799A]/13	HK to DLS	MCW/261
18/4/1938	17	HK/C/L/[799A]/14	DLS to HK	MCW/261
21/4/1938	18	HK/C/L/[799A]/15	HK to DLS	MCW/261
1/5/1938	19	HK/C/L/[799A]/16	DLS to HK	MCW/261

6/5/1938	20	HK/C/L/[799A]/17	HK to DLS	MCW/261
16/5/1938	21	HK/C/L/[799A]/18	DLS to HK	MCW/261
21/5/1938	22	HK/C/L/[799A]/19	HK to DLS	MCW/261
24/5/1938	23	HK/C/L/[799A]/20	HK to DLS	MCW/261
[24/5/1939]	24	HK/C/L/[799A]/8	HK to DLS	MCW/261
4/7/1938	25	HK/C/L/[799A]/21	DLS to HK	MCW/261
25/12/1938	26	HK/C/L/[799A]/22	HK to DLS	MCW/261
20/2/1939	27	HK/C/L/[799A]/24	DLS to HK	MCW/261
10/3/1939	28	HK/C/L/[799A]/23	HK to DLS	MCW/261
11/6/1939	29	HK/C/L/[799A]/25	HK to DLS	MCW/261
15/6/1939	30	HK/C/L/[799A]/26	DLS to HK	MCW/261
22/6/1939	31	HK/C/L/[799A]/27	HK to DLS	MCW/261
22/6/1939	32	HK/C/L/[799A]/28	DLS's Secretary to HK	MCW/261
2/7/1939	33	HK/C/L/[799A]/29	DLS to HK	MCW/261
6/7/1939	34	HK/C/L/[799A]/30	HK to DLS	MCW/261
19.9.1940	35	HK/C/L/799/6	DLS to HK	SSM
10/10/1940	36	HK/C/L/[799A]/31	HK to DLS	MCW/260
14/4/1941	37	HK/C/L/[799A]/32	HK to DLS	MCW/260
7/5/1941	38	HK/C/L/799/7	DLS to HK	SSM
11/5/1941	39	HK/C/L/[799A]/33	HK to DLS	MCW/260

15/5/1941	40	HK/C/L/799/8	DLS to HK	SSM
20/4/1944	41	HK/C/L/799/9	DLS to HK	SSM
15/8/1946	42	HK/C/L/[799A]/34	HK to DLS	MCW/260
8/3/1947	43	HK/C/L/[799A]/35	HK to DLS	MCW/260
10/7/1947	44	HK/C/L/[799A]/36	HK to DLS	MCW/260
24/7/1947	45	HK/C/L/[799A]/37	DLS to HK	MCW/260

Biographical Timelines

Herbert Hamilton Kelly

1860	Born in Manchester where his father, James Davenport Kelly, was rector of St James's, George Street. He was the third of seven children
1872–77	Manchester Grammar School
1878–79	Royal Military Academy, Woolwich
1879–83	Queen's College, Oxford (gained a fourth-class degree in history)
1884	Ordained priest
1883–90	Served in various parishes
	'it took me just over ten years to learn my utter uselessness – as a soldier (exit 1879), as a student (exit 1883), as a parish priest (exit 1890). Note how a man's *in*capabilities may direct his calling'.[1]
1890	Inspired by a call to send missionaries to Korea he established a small community, the Corean Missionary Brotherhood, in Vassall Road, London, to train aspirants
1893	Founded the Society of the Sacred Mission (SSM)
1896	SSM moved to Mildenhall, Suffolk
1898	Wrote the *History of a Religious Idea*
1901–2	*A History of the Church of Christ*
1902	*England and the Church*
1903	SSM moved to Kelham Hall, Nottinghamshire
1908	*An Idea in the Making*

---

[1] Quoted by Margaret Dewey, 'SSM Chronicle', p. 11.

1910	Retired as Director of SSM
1910–11	Involvement with Student Christian Movement camps at Edinburgh and Swanwick and visit to USA
1913	*The Church and Religious Unity*
1913–14 & 1916–19	In Japan
1920	Back at Kelham, teaching Dogmatics and Church History and writing his next two books. He continued his involvement with SCM and maintained a variety of interests including rock climbing and pig keeping
1928	*The Gospel of God*
1932	*Catholicity*
1937	Began correspondence with Dorothy L. Sayers
1950	Died at Kelham

Dorothy Leigh Sayers

1893	Born in Oxford where her father, Henry Sayers, was headmaster of Christ Church choir school and chaplain at the Cathedral
1898	Henry Sayers appointed Rector at Bluntisham, Cambridgeshire. Educated at home
1908	Godolphin School, Salisbury
1912–15	Somerville College, Oxford
1916–21	Teaching in various schools, published some early works
1922–31	Copywriter at H.S. Benson's advertising agency
1923	Published her first detective story *Whose Body?*
1924	Gave birth to a son, John Anthony (she and his father, Bill White, were unmarried and Sayers

	supported John Anthony throughout her life as his 'cousin')
1920s & 30s	Published her series of Peter Wimsey detective stories
1926	Married Oswald Atherton Fleming 'Mac'
1936	Her first play, *Busman's Honeymoon: A Detective Comedy in 3 Acts*, co-written with Muriel St Clare, opened at the Comedy Theatre, London
1937	*Zeal of Thy House*, written for the Canterbury Festival. Began correspondence with Herbert Kelly
1939	*The Devil to Pay*, written for the Canterbury Festival
1940	*The Man Born to Be King: A Play Cycle on the Life of Our Lord and Saviour Jesus Christ*. A twelve-episode BBC radio series broadcast between December 1941– October 1942
1940	*Creed or Chaos?*
1941	*The Mind of the Maker*
	Throughout the 1940s and 1950s she continued to publish theological essays
1949	Began her translation of Dante's *Divine Comedy*. The first canto, *Inferno* published
1950	Published the second canto *Purgatory*.
1957	Death – Sayers was still working on *Paradise* which was completed by Barbara Reynolds and published in in 1962.

Bibliography

Books

Anson, Peter, *The Call of the Cloister* (London: SPCK, 1959).

Bonhoeffer, Dietrich, *Life Together* (New York: Harper & Row, 1954).

Chesterton, G.K. *The Wisdom of Father Brown* (London: Cassell & Co., 1914).

Couldrey, Edmund, Preface, *Great and General Chapters 1894–1952* (London: SSM Press, 1950).

Every, George, *Christian Discernment* (London: Sheldon Press, 1940).

Every, George (ed.), *Herbert Kelly, No Pious Person: Autobiographical Recollections* (London: Faith Press, 1960).

Kelly, Herbert, *The History of a Religious Idea* (London: Simpkin & Co., 1889).

Kelly, Herbert, *A History of the Church of Christ*, volumes one and two (London: Longman & Co., 1901 & 1902).

Kelly, Herbert, *On the Aim and Methods of Theological Study*, (Kelham: SSM Press, 1903).

Kelly, Herbert, *England and the Church* (London: Longman & Co., 1902).

Kelly, Herbert, *An Idea in the Working* (Kelham: SSM Press, 1908).

Kelly, Herbert, *The Universities and Training for the Clergy* (London: Sherrat & Hughes, 1909).

Kelly, Herbert, *The Social Teaching of the Medieval Church* (London: Society of St Peter & St Paul, 1925).

Kelly, Herbert, *The Gospel of God* (London: SCM, 1929).

Kelly, Herbert, *Catholicity* (London: SCM, 1932).

> Copies of all editions of Herbert Kelly's published books and pamphlets are held in the SSM Archives at the Borthwick Institute (SSM/HK/PB). His unpublished papers, lectures etc. are also listed and stored in the collection (SSM/HK/UPW).

> A selection is also available on the website: https://herbertkelly.ssm.org.uk/writings.

> Bound volumes of the *SSM Quarterly Paper* to which Herbert Kelly contributed many articles may be consulted at SSM/S/QP.

Mason, Alistair, *History of the Society of the Sacred Mission* (Norwich: Canterbury Press, 1993).

Orczy, Emmuska, *The Scarlett Pimpernel* (London: Greening & Co. 1905).

Reynolds, Barbara (ed,) *The Letters of Dorothy L. Sayers,* volumes 2 and 3, (Cambridge: Dorothy L. Sayers Society, 1997).

Reynolds, Barbara, *Dorothy L. Sayers, Her Life and Her Soul* (London: Sceptre, 1998).

Rieger, Julius in Zimmermann, W-D and Smith, R. G: *I Knew Dietrich Bonhoeffer* (New York: Harper & Row, 1966, pp. 95-103).

Sayers, Dorothy L. *Unnatural Death* (London: Gollancz, 1927).

Sayers, Dorothy L. *Gaudy Night* (London: Gollancz, 1935).

Sayers, Dorothy L. *The Zeal of Thy House* (London: Gollancz, 1937).

Sayers, Dorothy L. *The Devil to Pay* (London: Gollancz, 1939).

Sayers, Dorothy L. *Strong Meat* (London: Hodder & Stoughton, 1939).

Sayers, Dorothy L. *Begin Here: A Wartime Essay* (London: Gollancz, 1940).

Sayers, Dorothy L. *The Mind of the Maker* (London: Methuen, 1941).

Sayers, Dorothy L. *The Man Born to be King* (London: Gollancz, 1944).

Sayers, Dorothy L. *Creed or Chaos?* (London: Methuen, 1947).

Sayers, Dorothy L. (trans.) *The Comedy of Dante: Cantica I: Hell* (Harmondsworth: Penguin, 1949).

Sayers, Dorothy L. (trans.) *The Comedy of Dante: Cantica II: Purgatory* (Harmondsworth: Penguin, 1955).

Sayers, Dorothy L. and Barbara Reynolds (trans.) *The Comedy of Dante: Cantica III: Paradise* (Harmondsworth: Penguin, 1957).

Sayers, Dorothy L. and Paton Walsh, Jill, *Thrones, Dominations*, (London: Hodder Paperbacks, 1998).

Stubbs, William (ed.), *The Historical Works of Gervase of Canterbury* (London: Longman & Co., 1880).

Wells, H.G. *God the Invisible King* (London: Cassell & Co., 1917).

Articles

Carter Wood, John, 'Going "part of the way together": Christian intellectuals, modernity and the secular in 1930s and 1940s Britain', *Contemporary British History*, 2020, pp. 580–602.

Draper, Peter, 'Interpretations of the Re-building of Canterbury Cathedral, 1174–1186: Archaeological and Historical Evidence', *Journal of the Society of Architectural Historians*, 56, 1997, pp. 184–203.

Gelin, Marie-Pierre, 'Gervase of Canterbury, Christ Church and the Archbishops', *Journal of Ecclesiastical History*, 60, 2009, pp. 449–63.

Lyon, David, 'The Idea of a Christian Sociology: Some Historical Precedents and Current Concerns', *Sociological Analysis*, Autumn 1983, Vol 44, pp. 227-42.

Reynolds, Barbara, 'Fifty Years On: Dorothy L. Sayers and Dante', *VII: Journal of the Marion E. Wade Center,* 16, 1999, pp. 3–6.

Schwartz, E., 'The Curious Case of Dorothy L. Sayers and the Jew Who Wasn't There', *Moment Magazine*, July/August 2016.

Wiedemann Hunt, Margaret, 'Playwrights are not Evangelists': Dorothy L. Sayers on Translating the Gospels into Drama', *Studies in Church History*, 53, 2017, pp. 405–19.

Willerton, Chris, 'Dorothy L. Sayers and the Creative Reader', *VII: Journal of Marion E. Wade Center*, 28, 2011, pp. 47–60.

Unpublished

Dewey, Margaret, 'SSM Chronicle'.

Jones, Alan Williams, 'Herbert Hamilton Kelly S.S.M. 1860–1950: A Study in Failure', University of Nottingham, 1971. (https://eprints.nottingham.ac.uk/27617/1/582153.pdf).

Kelly, Herbert, *Ad Fratres*, 1906
https://herbertkelly.ssm.org.uk/writings

Index

Printed in Dunstable, United Kingdom